NEGOTIATING THE
NEW START TREATY

NEGOTIATING THE NEW START TREATY

Rose Gottemoeller

Rapid Communications in Conflict and Security Series
General Editor: Geoffrey R.H. Burn

CAMBRIA
PRESS

Amherst, New York

Library of Congress Cataloging-in-Publication Data

Names: Gottemoeller, Rose E. (Rose Eilene), 1953- author.

Title: Negotiating the new START Treaty / Rose Gottemoeller.

Description: Amherst : Cambria Press, 2021. |
Series: Cambria rapid communications in conflict and security series | Includes index. |

Summary: "Rose Gottemoeller, the US chief negotiator of the New START treaty-and the
first woman to lead a major nuclear arms negotiation-delivers in this book an invaluable
insider's account of the negotiations between the US and Russian delegations in Geneva
in 2009 and 2010. It also examines the crucially important discussions about the treaty
between President Barack Obama and President Dmitry Medvedev, and it describes the
tough negotiations Gottemoeller and her team went through to gain the support of the
Senate for the treaty. And importantly, at a time when the US Congress stands deeply
divided, it tells the story of how, in a previous time of partisan division, Republicans
and Democrats came together to ratify a treaty to safeguard the future of all Americans.
Rose Gottemoeller is uniquely qualified to write this book, bringing to the task not only
many years of high-level experience in creating and enacting US policy on arms control
and compliance but also a profound understanding of the broader politico-military
context from her time as NATO Deputy Secretary General. Thanks to her years working
with Russians, including as Director of the Carnegie Moscow Center, she provides rare
insights into the actions of the Russian delegation-and the dynamics between Medvedev
and then-Prime Minister Vladimir Putin. Her encyclopedic recall of the events and
astute ability to analyze objectively, while laying out her own thoughts and feelings at
the time, make this both an invaluable document of record-and a fascinating story. In
conveying the sense of excitement and satisfaction in delivering an innovative arms
control instrument for the American people and by laying out the lessons Gottemoeller
and her colleagues learned, this book will serve as an inspiration for the next generation
of negotiators, as a road map for them as they learn and practice their trade, and as a
blueprint to inform the shaping and ratification of future treaties"-- Provided by publisher.

Identifiers: LCCN 2021002897 (print) | LCCN 2021002898 (ebook) |
ISBN 9781621966999 (library binding) | ISBN 9781621966951 (paperback) |
ISBN 9781621965978 (epub) | ISBN 9781621965961 (pdf)

Subjects: LCSH: Treaty between the United States of America and the Russian
Federation on Measures for the Further Reduction and Limitation of Strategic
Offensive Arms (2010 April 8) | Nuclear arms control--United States. | Nuclear
arms control--Russia (Federation) | United States--Foreign relations--
Russia (Federation) | Russia (Federation)--Foreign relations--United States.

Classification: LCC KZ5662.32 .G68 2021 (print) | LCC KZ5662.32 (ebook) |

DDC 327.1/7470973--dc23

LC record available at https://lccn.loc.gov/2021002897

LC ebook record available at https://lccn.loc.gov/2021002898

To Ray,
without whom this life
would not have been possible

TABLE OF CONTENTS

List of Figures

ACKNOWLEDGMENTS

My thanks for those who helped me with this book begin with George Shultz, the former U.S. Secretary of State. When I arrived at the Hoover Institution in January 2020, I paid him a call and told him I was planning to write a book on the New START negotiations. "What's your best advice for me?" I asked him. "Tell a story," he said, "that's what Ronald Reagan always did, and he always got his point across." So I have done my best to make this book a good story. Sadly, George Shultz has left us, but I will always be grateful to him for launching me into the writing process. I miss him.

The New START senior negotiating team is an incomparable group of people, and I am so grateful that Marcie Ries, Mike Elliott, Kurt Siemon, and Dick Trout were able to cast their eyes over the manuscript and give me their patient advice as well as so many funny anecdotes. While I was writing, I constantly thought of Ted Warner, who has also left us: I miss him too. I will always remember him as one of the chief architects of the New START Treaty.

A number of people who served on the delegation or in Washington stepped forward and helped to correct my faulty memory and fill in many details of delegation and interagency life. I really appreciated it when

Carolyn Pura assembled some of us in her Foggy Bottom townhouse for lunch and recollections: that was the day I got serious about this book project. Carolyn, along with Marshall Brown, Brandy Buttrick, Neil Couch, James Miller, David Rust, Lynn Rusten, and Jessica Zdravecky deserve special thanks for their close reading of the text and detailed comments. Cecile St. Julien helped me sort out the timing of the Geneva endgame and, as our delegation photographer, ransacked her photo library for me. I never got her gumbo recipe, though.

Two individuals deserve special thanks for their role in helping me to recollect the ratification process: Terri Lodge and Brian McKeon. They made sure that I got right the critical dates, the personalities, and the issues. It was nerve-wracking to spend weeks running up to the ratification vote in the Vice President's office on Capitol Hill, but Brian kept the fire burning (literally), and neither of them ever lost their cool.

Michael Gordon, another facet of the ratification tale, read my story of his role, and we had a good laugh about it. I think he enjoyed being linked to an act of God.

At the State Department, the Office of the Historian was enormously helpful in giving me the opportunity to read key materials that helped to refresh my memory and straighten out details of the narrative. Elizabeth Charles and James Wilson were always supportive, and I appreciated their last-minute help as the COVID-19 pandemic bore down on Washington and closed offices across the city. James, like Secretary Shultz, had excellent advice for me: "Just start writing."

The State Department's Office of Information Programs and Services was also responsive and thorough during the review process, ensuring careful interagency attention to the manuscript. I really appreciated Eric Stein's leadership and Behar Godani's attention to detail and patience with my many queries.

When I was tearing my hair trying to find photographs, Joe Harris of Absolutely Archives was able to produce them within a few hours or days, making sure that I had the requisite quality and proper credits. It goes to show that if you have a special job to do, you need a professional.

Speaking of photos, I would like to give special thanks to Brian Denver, Deputy Public Affairs Officer at the U.S. Mission in Geneva, who made an extra effort to find archived photos of the delegation that I could not otherwise lay my hands on. Likewise, I am grateful to Heather Moore, Photo Historian in the U.S. Senate Historical Office, who helped me track down another elusive shot.

My family also had some work to do in producing photographs from the family album and reading the chapters where they made an appearance. My sons Dan and Paul and nieces Megan and Hillary had a good time, they said, remembering their adventures in Switzerland in the summer of 1990. My husband Ray not only read several drafts but also helped with the recollections *and* proofreading. As usual, Ray went above and beyond the call of duty.

At Stanford, I have to post a big thank you to Michael McFaul, who was instrumental in bringing me to campus as Payne Distinguished Lecturer at the Freeman Spogli Institute. My good colleagues are too numerous to name, but they have been uniformly welcoming despite the pandemic year. To produce the book, I would not have survived without the daily help of my research assistant, Daniil Zhukov, who is the fastest fact-checker in Russian and English I have ever met. George Mason, who edited initial versions of the manuscript several times, taught me things about the English language I thought I already knew. I am deeply grateful to them both.

Finally, I want to recognize Cambria Press. From the very first day when I talked with Geoffrey Burn, General Editor of the Cambria Rapid Communications in Conflict and Security Series, I knew that I was dealing with a team of consummate professionals who understand modern book publishing inside and out. Toni Tan, Director of Cambria Press, was unfailingly patient with my gaffes during the process. David Armstrong, my editor, has been a pleasure to work with, as has Ben Goodman on the marketing side. To all at Cambria, thank you.

As always, I will wrap up these acknowledgements with the firm statement that any errors of fact or judgment in the book are strictly my own. I had many friends to help me, but I am the one who put it down on paper.

Disclaimer

The opinions and characterizations in this piece are those of the author and do not necessarily represent those of the U.S. government.

Prologue

In 1977, I got a job working as a Russian linguist at a satellite ground station in Fort Detrick, Maryland. The U.S.–Soviet hotline, which was put in place after the Cuban Missile Crisis so that U.S. and Soviet leaders could always communicate, had suffered some recent problems. Because it was originally a landline, farmers in Finland kept accidentally cutting through it with their plows. As a remedy, Washington and Moscow agreed to go to satellite links instead, with both U.S. and Soviet satellite networks involved.

I was at the U.S. ground station for the Soviet Molniya satellites, and my job was to ensure that if technical problems occurred, the satellite technicians could talk to each other. I had a huge teletype machine with a Cyrillic keyboard and got fast at typing messages on it, but I never dealt with the leaders of the United States and USSR. If President Jimmy Carter and Premier Leonid Brezhnev had actually needed to communicate during a crisis, then professional interpreters in the White House and the Kremlin would have done the job.

The operation was 24/7 so I learned what it was like to work a night shift, and I got to know a good deal about 1970s-era satellite technology. The techs I worked with were great. However, nuclear crises being scarce, the hotline was not much in use, so the job was among the most boring I ever had. I decided before too long that I needed to look elsewhere.

About that time, I heard that a Russian-speaking research assistant was needed at the RAND Corporation's office in Washington, DC. I did not know much about RAND, but I quickly found out that Thomas Wolfe, RAND's senior Soviet military analyst, was working on a book on the first Strategic Arms Limitation Talks, known as SALT I. He wanted someone who could read and analyze the Russian-language press and specialized journals.

I applied, got the job, and spent my first year at RAND immersed in Wolfe's project. He knew what he wanted: he made sure that I got a stack pass at the Library of Congress so that I could pore over the most obscure Soviet military journals. He thoroughly read my analyses, never failing to criticize if I got it wrong, but never stinting in his praise if I got it right. He also pushed me to write something early, which I did, a little RAND paper called "Soviet Arms Control Decision-making." He also pushed to get it published and went up against skeptical editors at RAND, who said that research assistants never got to publish just like that. In sum, Tom Wolfe was a great mentor.

After Wolfe's *The SALT Experience* came out in January 1979, I went on to other work at RAND, flourishing there for over a decade. Wolfe retired in the early 1980s, but I must say that working with him on the book was a formative experience for me. Thanks to him, I was launched on a nuclear policy career. I took the journeyman's path rather than the academic one, never acquiring a PhD. I came up in the research world with Russian language as my ticket, hitched to a keen interest in the technical aspects of nuclear weapons and their control, which Wolfe encouraged.

Forty years later, I am paying back my debt to Tom Wolfe by telling my own story about the negotiation of the New START Treaty. I hope that it will boost interest in nuclear arms control and the negotiating process to a wider audience, most especially younger people who might feel like "I will never be allowed" or "I will never be able to do that." I did not think so either in 1978, but here I am, negotiator of a strategic nuclear arms treaty. So I hope by this book to inspire and mentor new players in the nuclear policy game, wherever and whoever they may be.

An Insider's Tale

Since I was the chief U.S. negotiator, this book has the intimate perspective of an insider. I am telling first the story of the negotiations with the Russians—what Presidents Barack Obama and Dmitry Medvedev did to launch and shape the negotiations, who were the personalities, both Americans and Russians, who worked the details, and what were the ups and downs over the twelve months of talks.

I will also zero in on the critical second part of the negotiations: the work with U.S. senators to achieve ratification of the treaty. This process is a crucial constitutional function of the Senate. Before the president can give his final sign-off on a treaty—in other words, ratify it—a two-thirds majority or sixty-seven senators must give their advice and consent. This means that not only do they get to vote yea or nay, but they also have the opportunity to offer recommendations about how the treaty should be implemented. In the New START case, the senators took this responsibility seriously, so I think that this treaty had a model ratification process. It is one that offers up lessons for the future.

For those in the expert community who may think that I am playing a little fast and loose throughout with technical terms, I decided to tell the story in as plain a way as I could, so that a wide audience could understand what we were trying to accomplish. If my plain English misleads in any way, then I will take the blame. I was determined not to get bogged down in technical terms, abbreviations, and acronyms. Some are inevitable, however—warheads, reentry vehicles, delivery vehicles, launchers, telemetry, throw-weight—these terms and others we cannot escape. I do my best to explain them as I go, but I have also provided a glossary of terms as a cheat sheet for readers. I hope that they will not be as difficult to remember as the characters in a Tolstoy novel.

There is one other formative moment in my career that I want to take note of as we begin. In 1990, I took up an International Affairs Fellowship of the Council on Foreign Relations. These fellowships are venerable. They have launched many a think tanker and academic into government, and many government officials into academia. They are perfect yeast for our revolving-door system, by which those from the academic community become senior political appointees when a new president arrives on the scene, and then they return to the research world when the administration ends. They also allow career government officials to take a much-needed break to restore their intellectual capital, spending a year thinking and writing at university, often somewhere like Harvard or Stanford.

This system is unique in the world and, in my experience, much envied. Typically, young graduates elsewhere enter a Ministry of Foreign Affairs and spend their life there, without much opportunity to try other things. Those on the academic side of the divide, in turn, are stuck there, without much opportunity to serve in government. Many, many times I have heard from foreign colleagues that they envy our revolving-door system. It allows for new ideas to flow constantly in and out of government. Some are good and some are bad, but at least they are not stale.

My fellowship placement was on what was then called the Soviet Desk in the Department of State. Those I worked with became firm friends and lifelong colleagues. Alexander Vershbow, who later preceded me as deputy secretary general of NATO, was the head of the Soviet Desk and my boss. John Tefft, who went on to become ambassador to Lithuania, Georgia, Ukraine, and Russia, was his deputy. Victoria Nuland, who became the first female American ambassador to NATO and later the assistant secretary for European affairs, was also on the Soviet Desk, along with many others who became for a generation the core team on U.S. policy toward the former Soviet space.

My immediate supervisors were John Ordway and later Steven Pifer. All three of us became closely involved with nuclear policy toward Russia, Ukraine, and the other independent states after the Soviet collapse. Both Ordway and Pifer thought it was a good idea to send me out as a junior State Department representative to the talks then underway in Geneva to negotiate a Strategic Arms Reduction Treaty, which became known as START I.

I served two six-week stints in Geneva, the first in the summer of 1990 and the second in the winter of 1991. I quickly came under the wing of an experienced Army officer, Kurt Siemon, in the group working on the treaty text. Kurt showed me the ropes, almost immediately entrusting me with some tasks. Like Tom Wolfe before him, he guided me and let me know when I was barking up the wrong tree. He also pushed me forward to present my work, when he felt it was worthwhile, to my immediate boss, State Department senior representative Ed Ifft, and even to the delegation heads, Richard Burt and later Linton Brooks.

As a result, I was asked early on to present some questions to the Soviet delegation during a plenary session. As I recall, I had found some inconsistency in how they were using Russian-language terminology on missile silos. It seemed that we might have had different definitions in play, which can cause serious treaty problems. The Soviets were surprised that such a young person should be asked to speak, and a female at that. I do not remember that the Soviet team actually gave an answer to my questions, but at least we were alerted to the fact that certain definitions needed to be tightened. Good definitions agreed to by both sides are the absolute core of an effective arms control treaty.

I have long thought about whether a stunt that I pulled during my six-week summer stint was worth it. Of the generation who thought we could have it all—marriage, children, work, the "superwoman" ideal—I decided that I would take my two small sons with me to Geneva. My husband Ray

Arnaudo agreed, and so I asked my two college-age nieces, Megan and Hillary Gottemoeller, if they would like an expenses-paid summer trip to Europe. The catch was that they would have to watch the kids during the week while I was working, but they would be free on the weekends.

Siblings Megan and Hillary thought it was a great idea, and so all five of us went off to Geneva. My sons, however, were little—Dan was seven and Paul was three—so it was a strain on them. Paul started howling at any break in his routine, such as the time the girls tried to take him for lunch to some place besides McDonald's.

I, too, found it was a strain on me because I had not realized that delegation work extended far into the evenings and weekends. Before too long, I felt like the weak link on the negotiating team, slinking off every day to cook dinner and see the boys to bed, and staying away on weekends because I was caring for them. Megan and Hillary were great, taking Dan and Paul on many adventures, including letting Dan, the fearless seven-year-old, jump off a diving tower into Lake Geneva. Somehow, we all survived. I have wondered since if it was a good idea to try such a superwoman stunt, but the other four do not wonder—they say it bonded them for life. (See figure 1.)

Being on the U.S. START delegation was a lucky break for me. Without this experience, I would have had no idea how to go about organizing the team working on the New START Treaty in 2009. Kurt Siemon turned up to work on New START, this time as the senior representative of the Department of Energy, which was a fitting link back to the START talks both for me and for the wider delegation.

I stay deeply grateful to all those who pushed me during that fellowship year. That is the beauty of these International Affairs Fellowships—they let you try your wings. If you flop, it is not fatal, but if you succeed, you come away with good experience to take you forward.

FLOW AND STRUCTURE

The book begins on April 1, 2009, when President Obama and President Medvedev met in London and agreed to launch the negotiations for a treaty to follow on the Strategic Arms Reduction Treaty (START). It proceeds to the first encounters in Rome, Geneva, and Moscow, then moves to the presidential summit in the Kremlin in early July. After that, it accelerates through the rest of 2009—we were trying to complete the new treaty before START went out of force on December 5. In retrospect, it was mission impossible, but that was the presidents' instruction to us out of London. Then began the slog through the difficult winter and early spring of 2010 to complete the treaty by early April.

Immediately the story shifts to Capitol Hill, where we began working right away on the ratification process with the Senate. It was a serious business that brought into consideration nuclear force modernization, fissile material production, and national missile defense. These were all heavy budget and policy issues. In addition, the president had the political legacy of declaring in Prague in April 2009 that he was firmly committed to a world without nuclear weapons. Thus, his nuclear arms reduction aspirations went beyond the New START Treaty to additional treaties during his time in the White House. We were put on notice to get this treaty finished and into force so that we could move on quickly to the next one.

Life is full of the unpredictable, and New START was no exception. A freezing *bise* (cold wind) from the Alps encased Geneva in ice and many in both delegations fell ill. "Snowmageddon," a record snowfall in Washington, DC, in February, shut down the city at a critical phase in the talks. With limited means to communicate securely with colleagues stuck at home, the delegation received very few instructions for a week. The Russians looked on gleefully, reminding us that Moscow could easily keep operating in snow. During the ratification process, Wikileaks roared on the scene at a delicate phase, threatening to distract attention just as we were preparing for the Senate vote. These were events that I never could have predicted.

Personal lessons learned from the experience will round out my story. I had learned everything I knew about negotiating arms control treaties from my experience on the START delegation in 1990–1991. By 2009, however, the world had changed, and I had to think carefully, with my team, about how we could take advantage of technologies that had not been around for earlier negotiations. In 1990 we had fax and copying machines, but we did not have email. In 1990 we had secure telephones, but we did not have secure videoconferencing. In 1990, if you had a phone, it was on your desk, not in your pocket. All these advances—email, especially the classified variety, secure videoconferencing, and mobile phones—had a profound effect on the speed and conduct of the negotiations.

I am following in the footsteps of a generation of American and Russian negotiators who wrote about their experiences, sometimes in personal ways, sometimes in technical and detailed ways. They taught me everything that I know. Their memoirs tell the tale of a way of Americans and Russians working together to control, limit and reduce that most fearsome weapon of mass destruction, the nuclear bomb.

I hope my story will add to that proud legacy. Its roots are in Tom Wolfe's *The SALT Experience*, which brought me into the field of nuclear policy and arms control forty years ago. My aim for this book is that it will do the same, spurring people, young and old, to think about the opportunities and challenges of the field. In particular, my wish is that this book will inspire new negotiators to enter the game. As I always like to say, negotiating a nuclear treaty is not rocket science. It requires a clear-eyed sense of where U.S. national interest lies. Then, we must negotiate so that the treaty serves that interest. Plenty of people, most importantly in the Senate, will let you know if you succeed.

NEGOTIATING THE
NEW START TREATY

CHAPTER 1

FRAMING THE
NEW START TREATY

BUILDING CONSENSUS ON NUCLEAR ARMS CONTROL

The leaders of the United States and Russia were facing an important deadline in April 2008. The Strategic Arms Reduction Treaty, known as START, was going out of force in December of 2009, just over one year later. President George W. Bush and his administration were intent on replacing it with a new agreement, one that was not quite so complicated—more on the model of the so-called Moscow Treaty, which President Bush had signed with President Vladimir Putin in 2002. The Russians, for their part, agreed that START should be replaced, albeit with a different approach.

How did we get here? The priority that both sides put on replacing START in 2008 was important, but it was not always so. When President Lyndon Johnson first discussed nuclear arms control with Soviet Premier Alexei Kosygin in 1967, at Glassboro State College in New Jersey, he was met with incomprehension.

The Glassboro Summit was the first time that the United States presented to Soviet leaders the proposition that it is important to limit strategic ballistic missile defenses, as well as strategic nuclear offensive weapon systems. It is a simple argument: if strategic-strike offensive missiles are limited and ballistic missile defense systems continue to improve technologically and expand operationally, then over time, the defense systems will begin to undermine the strategic offensive deterrent of one party or the other.

The Soviet leaders were baffled: How could limiting defenses ever be a good thing? Premier Kosygin and his colleagues were no doubt confounded because Soviet military doctrine and strategy, including nuclear doctrine, were strictly the purview of the Soviet military leadership. It was probably the first time that the Communist Party leadership had ever heard anything about the nuclear offense-defense relationship.

By the time President Richard Nixon met in Moscow with Party General Secretary Leonid Brezhnev in May 1972, the Soviets were convinced of the need to limit defensive as well as offensive systems. President Nixon and Secretary Brezhnev signed the Anti-Ballistic Missile Treaty, which limited each side to 100 defensive launchers in two sites each. They also signed the Strategic Arms Limitation Treaty (SALT I), which was called an interim agreement because it simply froze the number of launchers then deployed. It did not contain any on-site inspection measures, which the Soviets were not yet ready to consider at their sensitive deployment sites. Instead, verification of SALT I depended on "National Technical Means" (NTM); that is, the satellites, radars, and reconnaissance aircraft that each side deployed to watch the other.

The Soviet decision to limit for the first time both offensive and defensive systems was significant. The same theme comes up again and again in the history of U.S.–Russian arms control policy: the delicacy of the offense-defense balance and the importance of maintaining it for the sake of strategic stability. Indeed, the balance plays a central role in this story of the New START Treaty.

Fast-forward to 1979 and the completion of SALT II, the first actual treaty that sought to limit strategic offensive arms. For the first time, the treaty enshrined "parity," or equality in terms of nuclear delivery vehicles, between the two parties. It never entered into force because of the Soviet invasion of Afghanistan in December that year; even without that complication, President Jimmy Carter was already facing an uphill battle in getting the advice and consent of the Senate to its ratification. The reason? U.S. hawks and skeptics were sharply criticizing what they called the Soviet breakout potential—the advent of MIRV technology.

MIRV stands for multiple independently targetable reentry vehicles, which allow a country to deploy multiple warheads on top of individual missiles. Because the Soviets were deploying heavy missiles—the SS-18 and SS-19 ICBMs—they had more capability to carry and deliver warheads. This was the famous "throw-weight" debate of the 1970s and 1980s. It was feared that the Soviets had enormous potential to deploy and deliver many more warheads than the United States could, thereby upsetting the strategic balance. Although SALT II attempted to limit MIRV technology, it was not enough for the critics.

Of course, two can play this game. Within a short time, the United States was also deploying very capable MIRVs on its ground-based systems, the ICBMs, but more so on its submarine-based systems, the sea-launched ballistic missiles (SLBMs). During this era, the United States maintained much quieter submarines and was able to deliver more accurate strikes from sea-based platforms than the Soviets. The Soviets thus had cause to consider what would happen should the United States choose to deploy an unlimited number of highly accurate warheads at sea, where they could not be easily tracked and targeted.

MIRV technology thus became the real impetus for the two sides to agree in the 1980s to Strategic Arms Reduction Talks. It had proved futile to try to *limit* strategic systems; they had to be *reduced* and in such a way that each side could be certain that one would not be able to out-deploy the other in warhead numbers.

That is why they worked hard and long to negotiate START, which finally entered into force in 1994. It constrained nuclear delivery vehicles and their launchers, as well as the warheads deployed on them. It also, for the first time in a strategic arms treaty, included on-site inspections. The Russians had finally decided that the value of having access to U.S. nuclear missile facilities outweighed their concerns about granting such access to American inspectors.

Thus, by 1994, the two sides shared a consensus that nuclear arms control had become a valuable component of their national security. Verifiable arms control treaties, especially once on-site inspections were agreed, meant more predictability, the understanding of what kinds of nuclear weapons the other side was deploying, where they were deployed, in what numbers, and at what level of readiness.

This understanding, in turn, allowed each side to bound the costs of its own nuclear arsenal. Both sides were able to conclude that they would need to modernize their nuclear arsenals only rarely. In 2020, the Russian Federation was just completing the modernization of its intercontinental ballistic missile force, replacing SS-18 and SS-19 missiles that the USSR had first deployed in the 1970s and 1980s. The United States was just beginning to modernize its Ohio-class strategic submarine force, a replacement effort that will not be completed until the 2030s. The Ohio SSBN, the first in the class, was launched in 1979.

The treaties limit numbers, allowing each side to predict the size of the other's arsenal, at least for the life of the treaty. Thus, under New START, the United States knows that it does not need to build and deploy more than 700 strategic missiles or bombers, and the same goes for the Russian Federation. In this way, control of nuclear weapons prevents arms racing.

WHY NUCLEAR MODERNIZATION?

As Russia completes its nuclear modernization and the United States embarks on its own, the question occurs, why not let these dreadful weapons just die a natural death? There are a number of reasons why they need to be replaced. One is safety: as weapon systems age, they become more prone to accidents. If an accident occurs, they must not detonate—they must be fail-safe. The launch platforms must also be safe. Some of the older Soviet platforms, especially the submarines, were radioactive death traps and needed to be replaced as soon as possible for the sake of their crews.

Another reason is security. If the wrong person, a terrorist, or rogue actor, gets his hands on a weapon, he must not be able to explode it. Hollywood has made much of such scenarios, especially since the breakup of the USSR created concerns that its nuclear warheads may find their way into the black market and be sold to the highest bidder. Both the United States and Russia treat nuclear security very seriously. We even worked closely together in the first two decades after the Soviet demise to ensure the security of Russian nuclear weapons and materials.

Finally, both countries care about effectiveness: as weapon systems age, they may no longer perform as designed. Nuclear weapons, to be an effective deterrent, must detonate as planned should the terrible day ever arise when they are needed. That means they must sustain their effectiveness over a long period of time and in difficult deployment settings such as submarines in the deep ocean or ICBM silos in the icy tundra.

Despite emphasizing nuclear disarmament in his speech at Prague Castle in 2009, Barack Obama cited the importance of these three issues. He said that as long as nuclear weapons exist, the United States must maintain a safe, secure, and effective arsenal. This reasoning underpinned his decision to proceed with a nuclear modernization in 2017, before he left office.

The price tag for this modernization has risen to well over $1 trillion—an expensive proposition that has attracted a fair amount of criticism to President Obama. However, the modernization is constrained by the limits now in place under the New START Treaty—700 delivery vehicles,

800 launchers, and 1,550 warheads. Likewise, despite the fact that the Russians are building and deploying new nuclear weapon systems, including a new heavy missile, the Sarmat, and a new hypersonic glide weapon, the Avangard, they will not deploy more than the limits of New START allow. They must choose how many of the new missiles will replace their highly reliable mobile ICBMs, which they have also recently modernized. Once again, nuclear arms control has bounded the problem, preventing unpredictable spikes in numbers and arms racing.

Both the U.S. and Russian militaries value this nuclear predictability because they can avoid unpleasant nuclear surprises. It frees them up to modernize their conventional forces; they rarely need to think about nuclear weapons. They can add new conventional capabilities that take advantage of the latest advances in technology. By contrast, nuclear weapons are old technology—seventy years old. They are weapons of mass destruction (WMDs) so they must be carefully managed, but they are for deterrence purposes and unlikely ever to be used.

If either the U.S. or Russian military has an extra dollar or ruble to spend, no doubt they would do so on advanced conventional weapons, which add value on the modern battlefield. No doubt they would also argue for training and advancing armed forces personnel, ensuring that they are paid and housed, and their healthcare is covered. All this costs money that is better spent in areas other than nuclear weapons.

Thus, nuclear arms control, in addition to the moral arguments that accrue to it, has practical, day-to-day utility for U.S. and Russian military forces. Its value added is in keeping nuclear weapons limited so that scarce defense budget resources can go to the conventional side of the ledger. Evidently, both the United States and Russia agree on this. It has cemented their commitment to pursue further strategic arms limitations.

Replacing START

Facing a deadline—START's demise in December 2009—President Bush and President Putin agreed that the treaty needed to be replaced, but they took different roads to do so. The Bush team was looking for a less complicated approach than START, and they proposed a replacement that would be simple and flexible. They based their proposal on the 2002 Moscow Treaty, also known as the Strategic Offensive Reduction Treaty (SORT). Moscow had a single limit on operationally deployed warheads—in a range from 1,700 to 2,200. Limits on delivery vehicles such as missiles and their launch platforms were not included.

The single warhead limit made sense when the Moscow Treaty was agreed because START remained in force and it *did* contain limits on delivery vehicles and their launchers. The two treaties fit together in continuing to reduce and limit nuclear weapon systems. Once START went out of force, the Bush administration seemed to feel confident that a single limit on warheads would be effective enough to continue the arms control process.

The Russian Federation did not agree. The Russians insisted that the new treaty should continue the START approach, with limits on delivery vehicles, launchers, and their warheads. They argued that the fundamental provisions of START should be carried forward into the new treaty, including verification measures, which the Bush team was proposing to forgo. The Russians stated point-blank that the U.S. proposal was not consistent with what Presidents Bush and Putin had signed up for during their summit in April 2008, when they agreed to reduce strategic offensive nuclear arms to "the lowest possible level." In fact, the Russians complained that the U.S. proposal contained no reductions at all.

Both the United States and Russia agreed that the START Treaty needed to be replaced, but they had very different concepts on how to do it. The Russians nailed themselves to the START mast, insisting that it determine the basis of the new treaty. The Bush administration was intent on a simpler, more flexible approach that would not insist on a tough verification regime or, indeed, on further reductions. Their proposal was designed more to maintain mutual confidence rather than pursue further nuclear reductions. In this way, the stage was set for the arrival of Barack Obama in office in January 2009.

BIPARTISAN SUPPORT AND PRESIDENTIAL LEADERSHIP

The U.S.-Russian bilateral consensus to extend START was important when Bush left office in January 2009, but so too was a *bipartisan* consensus in the United States that START needed to be replaced. The Republicans were pursuing a new treaty, although they were not friends of arms control diplomacy. In fact, one of the Bush administration's signal acts had been to withdraw from the Anti-Ballistic Missile (ABM) Treaty in June 2002. This action fueled Russian angst over the offense-defense relationship, which played out constantly in the ensuing years, including during the negotiation of the New START Treaty. Despite this history, President Bush was ready to replace START with a new treaty.

President Obama could naturally pick up on the issue as a bipartisan goal. An added impetus was his early focus on nuclear disarmament. In his April 2009 Prague speech, Obama called for "the peace and security of a world without nuclear weapons." Although the president properly caveated the goal of total nuclear disarmament—he said that it was a goal that would not be achieved in his lifetime—he did convey that he would seek to secure several nuclear arms reduction treaties in his administration. The first would be a quick replacement of START, but further treaties would be focused on achieving deeper and deeper reductions and on taking other steps to move toward nuclear disarmament. This effort came to be called Obama's Prague Initiative.

President Obama and President Medvedev arrived in London on April 1, 2009, meeting just four days prior to the Prague speech. Medvedev had replaced Putin as president in May 2008, with Putin stepping aside to become Russian prime minister. Now we know that Medvedev's time in office was a four-year interregnum, with Putin returning to the Russian presidency in 2012. At the time of the London meeting, however, it seemed that Russia might be on a new path with a new man in power. Perhaps the promise of a better relationship, hoped for since the breakup of the Soviet Union twenty years prior, would finally be borne out.

In this spirit, President Obama and his team offered the famous Russian "reset" button to President Medvedev at the London meeting. The gesture was a triumph of hope over the eventual reality, but it was certainly the right move to set the stage for the New START negotiations. Because London put the overall relationship on a more positive course, the talks were launched in a generally cooperative environment. Both sides received clear marching orders from the highest level, the presidents, that the treaty needed to get done, and quickly. START was going out of force in December 2009, only eight months away. The new treaty had to be finished by that time.

One of the funnier gaffes in summit history is that our Russian translation of "reset" was wrong. Instead of "reset" (*perezagruzka*), the Americans offered *peregruzka*, which means to overload, like to overload an electrical circuit. When I first arrived in Geneva to open the negotiations, the Russians had a fun time needling us about this mistake. I decided to go right along with them. I said that indeed the relationship had been bad in recent years, overloaded with many problems. The presidents had done the right thing to reset it in London. After a few days, the Russians let the joke go. We were too busy to let it trouble us further.

London produced two important documents, one a broad statement of the goals of the reset and the other a narrow statement of the goals of the new treaty negotiations. The broad statement covered security issues and, in particular, laid out an agenda for discussing our differences over the role of missile defenses and their potential impact on strategic offensive forces. The Russians continued to obsess about this issue, especially after the Bush administration's announcement of its intent to deploy missile defense facilities in NATO European countries. The Obama administration would be doing its own review of this deployment plan and would make some adjustments. However, the United States already clearly intended to build some missile defense sites in Europe not to defend against Russia but rather against limited missile threats, especially from Iran.

Discussions on this issue with the Russians were to be kept strictly separate from the negotiations to reduce strategic offensive forces. Ellen Tauscher, undersecretary of state for arms control and international security, would lead those discussions. She would try to convince the Russians of the true nature of the limited U.S. defense deployments as well as the potential to cooperate in this arena.

As for the new treaty, the narrow statement that the two presidents agreed on that day stressed three points that decisively shaped the negotiations. First, the subject of the new agreement would be strategic offensive arms; second, the parties would seek reductions below the level of the 2002 Moscow Treaty, which had lowered warhead numbers from 6,000 to 2,200; and third, the agreement would include effective verification measures that drew on the experience of START. The clear signal to the Russians was that the Bush proposal from October 2008, which did not call for further reductions or effective verification, was being superseded.

Crucially, the two presidents decided in London that the new treaty would *not* limit missile defenses but would reduce strategic *offensive* nuclear weapons, as START had done. That President Medvedev agreed to this approach at the time is fascinating because it evidently was not a settled issue in the Russian bureaucracy. In fact, it came up again and again during the negotiations. Because of this clear initial guidance, however, we were able to hold firm in the months that followed.

The presidents also specified that they intended to conclude the new agreement before START expired in December 2009—unprecedented speed for a nuclear arms reduction negotiation. Remarkably, the two presidents were of one mind: they needed to get a nuclear arms control treaty done—and quickly. Neither wanted to face a vacuum with no nuclear arms control treaty in force between the United States and the Russian Federation. They knew the goal was ambitious because previous arms control agreements had taken years to negotiate. START itself had taken almost six years, on and off, to be finished.

Negotiation of a new strategic arms reduction treaty was thus a policy priority for both men. President Obama was keen to negotiate what he hoped would be the first of a series of nuclear arms reduction treaties to pursue what he would lay out in Prague that same month—the goal of a world without nuclear weapons. Medvedev had taken over as Russian president from Putin just a year prior and was no doubt looking for a way to bolster his authority in the role. Neither he nor the Russian government was particularly invested in the Obama Prague Initiative, which we found out in the months that followed.

Despite these differences, the stage was well-set in London for negotiation of the new treaty.

Chapter 2

The Talks Take Shape

Setting the Negotiating Table

Secretary of State designate Hillary Clinton interviewed me to be the chief negotiator of the new treaty at a January 2009 meeting in a borrowed apartment high above Central Park in New York City. She was talking to a number of potential appointees during this period (I ran into another Washington denizen on Amtrak who ended up at the Treasury Department). I did not really know Secretary Clinton at that point, so I did not know what to expect, but I was nervous—and for good reason. Secretary Clinton was accompanied by her two incoming deputies, James Steinberg, an old friend, who was knowledgeable about nuclear weapons, and Jack Lew, whom I didn't know. I had heard Lew would be handling more the economic portfolio than security policy. In the end, all three of them peppered me with questions about nuclear deterrence, the U.S. nuclear triad, Russian doctrine, and how I would structure a new agreement. I left both exhausted and starving. I went to a diner and had a beer and large hamburger, then got back on Amtrak to go home. I was convinced that I hadn't done well.

The next day, however, I got a call from Secretary Clinton's assistant asking if I would be willing to speak to her. The house being full of raucous family members, I went out on the back deck in the cold to take the call. Secretary Clinton told me that she would like me to lead the negotiation of the new treaty and serve as the assistant secretary responsible for arms control. Would I be interested? My answer was a definite yes.

I was not in London for the April 1 meeting because the U.S. Senate had not yet confirmed me. Confirmation, with ratification, is another constitutional role for the Senate that is vital for U.S. institutions. Senator Richard Lugar, ranking Republican on the Senate Foreign Relations Committee (SFRC), had been pushing the process and he was clear with his Republican colleagues that they should not hold me up. My confirmation was a priority. Senator Lugar from the outset was a true leader on New START, and his role grew steadily as we sought his advice throughout the negotiations and ratification process. On April 4, three days after the London meeting, my confirmation came through.

With the basic parameters set in London, the early substantive work was done. The first task that I had to take on was to get the negotiating team up and running. I was exceedingly glad that Marcie Ries, who had been the U.S. ambassador in Albania and had just returned from Iraq, was willing to join as the senior representative from the Department of State. Although I came into the game as a political appointee from the State Department, as chief negotiator I had to work equally well with all the agencies and represent their interests in the talks with the Russians. Therefore, it was crucial to have a senior diplomat who would fully represent State Department interests. Marcie, with her long experience and excellent contacts, was just that person. She later became my principal deputy assistant secretary, or "PDAS" in State Department jargon.

On the Department of Defense side, I was equally delighted that Ted Warner became the secretary of defense's senior representative. We had worked together for years, starting at the RAND Corporation in Washington, DC, in the 1980s, where our offices were next to one another.

Ted had served as air attaché in Moscow, and so he knew the Russians and their weapon systems well. He was also one of the most relentlessly detail-oriented people I had ever met, so I knew he would be a great asset on highly technical treaty matters. Importantly, Ted was flexible and creative: when something wasn't working, Ted was always willing to look for new ideas.

Michael (Mike) Elliott, who was to represent the Joint Chiefs of Staff (JCS), was an unknown quantity because he had spent most of his U.S. Air Force career not in Washington but flying in bombers or working at the U.S. Strategic Command and its predecessors in Omaha. At the beginning, the old treaty hands worried that Mike was already retired from the U.S. Air Force and therefore wouldn't have the "reach back" that would be needed to call up senior uniformed leaders. In the end, nothing was further from the truth: he always got to the chairman of the Joint Chiefs of Staff when we needed him, as well as to his deputy and the service commanders, and anyone else in uniform.

Richard (Dick) Trout represented the Defense Department, and I was very glad indeed to have him on the delegation. He had a wealth of experience from previous negotiations and, most crucially, had worked at high levels with the Bush administration. He understood how to prepare for Russian mischief, as when they tried to turn back the clock to the October 2008 Bush administration proposal that they had previously discarded. I was truly grateful for his savvy and for his willingness to take the initiative and innovate.

Last but not least was Kurt Siemon, who had been my mentor when I arrived at the START negotiations in Geneva in 1990. During the New START talks, Kurt was the senior figure from the Department of Energy. His experience was so valuable because, unlike the rest of us, he had worked on negotiating START from the ground up. He understood how to write a clear definition or notification, which are highly technical and also potentially highly damaging to the success of a treaty if they are not right. He understood the role of telemetry in START and how that role could be different in the New START Treaty. I considered Kurt my "senior counselor" on the delegation and sought his advice on such technical matters.

This interagency negotiating team was backed up by very capable experts from each of their agencies. I am often asked if we were at a disadvantage because it had been over twenty years since the START negotiations concluded and many of the experienced hands on that delegation were retired. Where was I going to get my negotiators? First, I was lucky that there were still some old hands around who were willing to return to Geneva. The State Department was especially rich in them. Among our linguists all were exceptionally experienced, but some had worked on START twenty years prior and knew perfectly the ins and outs of treaty interpreting—including Russian foibles. So we were not completely bereft of experienced hands.

Second, and equally importantly, the agencies sent to Geneva experts who had participated in inspections of Soviet and Russian nuclear facilities, or who knew U.S. weapon systems well, having served in the U.S. Air Force or U.S. Navy on nuclear platforms. We also had a number of experts from the intelligence community who knew Russian weapon systems well. Although these individuals may never have sat at a formal negotiating table, they turned out to be natural negotiators whose deep technical knowledge earned the respect of their Russian counterparts. That is one reason why I do not worry today when people ask me, "Where will the negotiators come from for the next negotiation?" As long as the United States continues to deploy nuclear weapons and continues to conduct inspections at Russian facilities, there will be experts in our government who can step forward into the role of negotiators.

The backstoppers in Washington comprise the other crucial part of any negotiation; their role is to ensure that the team in Geneva is provided with timely guidance. This is more complicated than it sounds, because when talks really get going, the action can be very fast at the negotiating table, and the interagency process in Washington cannot keep up. The lead delegation members in such cases spend a lot of time on the phone or exchanging emails with their counterparts in Washington, explaining the logic and talking through the substance. The experts also get into the act, explaining technical details and describing how the details fit into the treaty constraint system. Washington would have to be sold on what we were trying to accomplish.

In the end, I think of the relationship between backstoppers and delegation as symbiotic, with constant feedback between the two. The importance of staying in close touch with the capital cannot be overstated, as I learned to my peril in the course of the year. The Russians, by the way, had a very similar feedback system, although their less free-flowing communications with Moscow—they were not allowed to use email— meant that they had to physically return to "home base" from time to time to explain what was going on in Geneva. This too created some heartburn later in the negotiations.

During the course of the negotiations, the backstopping interagency group in Washington was led first by George Look, who was the senior director for arms control and nonproliferation on the National Security Council staff, and then by Lynn Rusten, who succeeded George Look as senior director. Rusten came from the Senate Armed Services Committee staff following a senior stint in the Arms Control and Disarmament Agency. Both were superb: experienced, well-connected, detail oriented, and tough. Rusten's experience on Capitol Hill also made her the perfect person to lead interagency support for the ratification process, which had characteristics similar to treaty backstopping.

The backstopping group focused more on technical matters than on political ones, although the line of division was never absolute. Political guidance to the delegation normally came from a high-level group led by Gary Samore, who was the White House coordinator for arms control and weapons of mass destruction, and Michael McFaul, senior director and special assistant to the president, this time for Russian and Eurasian affairs. Ultimately, President Obama's interest in the matter was intense, so the cabinet itself engaged in giving guidance on a regular basis, especially at difficult moments in the negotiations. During those times, National Security Advisor James Jones and Deputy National Security Advisor Thomas Donilon were regularly involved, chairing the so-called "principals'" and "deputies'" meetings.

At the State Department, I had a regular line of communication with Secretary Clinton, through my "negotiator's notes" on an almost daily basis. Deputy Secretaries James Steinberg and Jack Lew wanted to be informed regularly of progress or problems. My immediate boss, Undersecretary Ellen Tauscher, was a vital link to Clinton when we needed her help, as we did on several crucial occasions. Tauscher also played a vital role in the negotiation endgame, where her skills as a natural negotiator came into vivid play. Undersecretary for Political Affairs William Burns, who had recently returned from being ambassador to Moscow, was an invaluable line of communications with the Russians and source of advice about the games they were up to. With his long experience dealing with Moscow, Burns ensured that we did not get tangled up in intra-Russian rivalries.

The key early message to me in setting the negotiating table was that President Obama was watching, would continue to pay attention, and wanted this negotiation done in time to replace the START Treaty when it went out of force in December 2009. This treaty was to be a first step in implementing his Prague Initiative, to achieve a world without nuclear weapons. We were on a tight deadline, and everyone knew it. We were lucky that no one, including the press, examined the deadline too closely, because if they did, they would have concluded early on that we were embarked on a mission impossible. To negotiate a major arms control treaty, achieve its ratification, and have it ready to enter into force within nine months had never been attempted before. With the best political will on both sides, and in the Senate, it was going to be difficult. But because no one looked too closely at what we were trying to do, we were left in peace to give it our best shot.

Tough-Girl Negotiator

Given the tight timeline, it was lucky that the negotiators of the New START Treaty knew each other so well. I had just come back from three years in Moscow working as director of the Carnegie Moscow Center. My counterpart, Anatoly Antonov, was director of the Arms Control and Disarmament Directorate in the Ministry of Foreign Affairs, and so we had encountered each other at Moscow think tank events. He even invited me to join his arms control advisory council, telling me afterwards that the decision had been controversial and that he had had to push back against criticism for allowing a foreign expert to join. From time to time, we had lunch and talked about the ins and outs of U.S. and Russian arms control policy, both nuclear and conventional, at the end of the second Bush administration.

Our acquaintance was one important factor in why the New START Treaty negotiations went so quickly. We never had to spend time on the "getting-to-know-you" dance of international negotiators, figuring out the basics of each other's personality and style. I knew him as an experienced diplomat and longtime participant in international nonproliferation, arms control and export control regimes; he knew me as a nongovernmental expert, albeit one who had a lot of experience working in Russia. I had also spent considerable time in Russia as a Clinton administration official during the early post-Soviet period, when we were cooperating to strengthen the protection of Russian nuclear materials and warheads against theft and terrorists. So to begin with, we had a wary mutual respect. (See figure 2.)

That mutual respect was almost upended, though, by the "tough-girl negotiator" incident. After the April meeting of the presidents, we were driving a hard pace to complete the new treaty. As we entered June and were preparing for a July encounter between Presidents Obama and Medvedev, a Russian newspaper published an article claiming that Antonov would never get the better of me because I was such a tough negotiator.

My heart sank when I read the piece because it was clear someone in Moscow was taking aim at Antonov. Not only was the other negotiator tougher than he, but she was a girl. Misogyny is a key feature of the Russian system, so it was a slap. I feared that, at worst, the article was a signal that Antonov was about to be replaced, and we would suffer inevitable delays as a new Russian negotiator was named and we started over to develop a working relationship. At best, I knew it would signal some weeks of gamesmanship from Antonov as he made it clear that he could be tough—tougher than I—at the negotiating table.

I am glad to say that it was the second outcome, although the weeks it took to get over the incident were not pleasant. When the presidents met in Moscow in July, Antonov took measures to cut me out of a key meeting with them. He then gleefully announced to the two delegations when we returned to the plenary meeting table that only he had been present at that crucial meeting and would have to report because I could not do so. On another early occasion in Geneva, I had invited him to a lunch, which is normal practice: from time to time, the negotiators meet for informal discussions over lunch or coffee. It was my first such invitation, and he agreed, but then took his time showing up. Fifty minutes late, he sauntered in and apologized with a flimsy excuse.

I think he expected me to storm out before he arrived, or after he'd given his flimsy excuse. Instead, I calmly said we had better order and we got on with lunch. He never turned up late to my invitation again, and we used our informal lunches and coffees to good effect in the negotiations, often breaking through conceptual or procedural logjams. Like other negotiators before us, we made good use of paper napkins to sketch on.

Reflecting on this period in the negotiations, I think we got through the games more quickly because I did not overreact. I can't say I liked being kept out of a key presidential meeting—normally that is a big blow to the authority of a negotiator—but I worked with the White House to ensure they knew I needed to be included in the future. It was never a problem again. At the same time, my calm reaction allowed Antonov to take early wins that were meaningless to the substance or progress of the talks.

On the contrary, as the pace picked up, our ability to interact very directly, with mutual humor and even jokes, made a big difference in keeping the day-to-day level of tension down across the two negotiating teams. Antonov told me several times that he relished playing games, so I took that into account in my own way: two can play. In my case, it took the form of reaching out to his back row.

In any negotiation, the leads are seated at the table: the two negotiators and the most senior people from the agencies that are working with them. Antonov had a similar set. In the back row are the experts—those who know the weapon systems inside and out, inspectors who know verification procedures, lawyers who understand treaty law, and linguists. Of course, the lead interpreter always sits next to the chief negotiator.

Early on, I realized that Antonov had an excellent team of young women on his delegation. In fact, he took pride in telling me that he had selected the best young female diplomats to participate—at the same time complaining that he couldn't get enough men because they were not going into the Foreign Ministry but into banking and business instead. All the women were sitting in the back row, along with other top experts from the Russian agencies. I decided I would do my best to encourage his back row, especially the women in it.

I started out conveying my own expertise, to message that women could do nuclear policy just as well as men. I used early plenary sessions to give detailed tutorials about how capable Russian missiles were and how Moscow, therefore, did not need to worry about U.S. missile defenses. These had the added advantage of showing that I knew a lot about technical topics—there were nods from the Russian military experts.

Later, I started reaching out to the women more directly. In December, I gave each of them a White House Christmas ornament, and when February came, there were the beads. One of our delegation members hailed from Louisiana, and for fun she had Mardi Gras beads shipped out to the delegation. I sent a basket of them down to the Russian Mission, prominently labeled "for the women on the Russian delegation." At that point, Antonov complained that I was showing unfair attention to the female side of his team. "Where are my beads?" he demanded.

I told him right along that he needed to let some of the capable female experts on his delegation into the front row and that they should be allowed to speak. Finally, toward the end of the negotiations, it happened. He announced that his female lawyer would be given a speaking role at the next plenary session. When she appeared in the front row that day and he turned to her, she exclaimed, "At last I get to speak!" Then she launched into a good sum-up of some legal business that we were bringing to conclusion.

One mistake I made in this campaign was to respond to a dinner invitation involving the women on his delegation. We did give and receive dinner invitations from time to time, and I thought it would be a chance to lend continuing support to the Russian women. No way. I dropped into the dinner late, when it was well underway, at a Thai restaurant not too far from the Russian Mission. It was evident that Antonov was behaving in a typical Russian way, dispensing drinks, giving toasts, and waxing lyrical about the special role that women play as the nurturers and supporters of men. He pounced on my arrival to pay some elaborate compliments to me in a similar vein. There were not a few grim smiles around the table. I soon made my apologies and left, reflecting that it would be a while before women would rise in the Russian diplomatic corps. My little games were fun for them, maybe, but I wasn't going to change their reality.

As I reflect on the "tough-girl negotiator" incident, I think part of it was inevitable. No woman had ever led a negotiation about nuclear arms reduction in the fifty-year history of U.S. and Soviet/Russian negotiations. The fact was going to attract comment, and it was going to rouse discomfort. The Russian discomfort I fully expected. In the end,

Antonov and I were able to work through it, and he showed himself to be the capable, experienced, and well-connected diplomat that he is.

I did not expect the same reaction on the U.S. side of the table, but I have to admit that I had to deal with some of it. While we were still in the early plenary exchanges, my delegation pushed me several times in confidential preparatory meetings to show more anger, to be tougher on the Russians. I was keeping to my own way: talking reasonably and delivering my lectures to the Russians, but the men wanted to see some temper. So one day, I decided to comply.

It was an early plenary meeting, and the Russians were continuing to push the notion that they needed missile defense constraints in the new treaty. They had already been trying, but I always had the same message in response: President Obama and President Medvedev had agreed in London in April that this negotiation was going to be about strategic *offensive* forces, not missile defense, period.

This time, I engaged in some street theater. I brought my hand down hard on the table and shouted, "President Obama and President Medvedev agreed in London in April that this negotiation is going to be about strategic *offensive* forces, not missile defense!" I heard afterward that I turned bright red in the bargain. The tantrum had its desired effect: the Russians were surprised, but more importantly, the men in my delegation were jubilant—she could pound the table when she needed to!

I got many compliments in the final team meeting that day. Most importantly, I didn't need to throw another tantrum for the rest of the negotiations. It was sufficient that I had proven I could do it if I had to. Male negotiators have many styles, some more histrionic, others more measured. I was able to show that women negotiators have the same range, although if I don't have to blow up, I won't.

CHAPTER 3

ROME—THE RED BALLROOM

THE NOSE TOUCH

Once we got started, I was eager to test whether the Russian side had taken the same message away from the London meeting that we had—to ensure we were on the same page as the negotiations began. I started talking to Gary Samore and George Look at the White House about what I called a "nose touch" with the Russians, in order to engage early, even while we were putting in place the details of our negotiating team and strategy.

Because I had known Antonov in Moscow, I felt at ease calling him on the phone and talking about the idea of an early meeting. We proposed it should be in Rome on April 24, the site of previous meetings that he had had with my predecessor, Paula DeSutter, and a place where I knew he was going to be anyway on Non-Proliferation Treaty (NPT) business. I wanted to make sure that the first meeting was convenient and low-key, and that we would not get into a kabuki dance about who was inviting whom and who "won" on proposing the first venue for talking.

Throughout the negotiations, I did my best to ease the machinations of negotiations: who's proposing, who's accepting, who's picking up the phone first, who's refusing to respond. It's normal negotiating behavior, but time consuming and, as we've already seen, Antonov loved to play games. I knew that we did not have much time and that the president was watching, so whenever I could, I looked for ease and speed in making arrangements. That often meant looking for convenience for the Russians; if it didn't make any difference to me or to our side, then I was fine with it.

I always assumed that the Russians were listening to phone calls made on an open line, including from Department of State phones. If I needed to say something confidential, I would use a secure line. I had spoken on an open line to my White House colleagues in the first days of April about the idea of a "nose touch." Within a few days, I called Antonov in Moscow to speak to him about the idea. He said to me in Russian, which we used sometimes in conversation, that he liked the expression "nosiki trogat"—in English, "to touch noses." He was showing me that he could listen in on my conversations, which in normal circumstances is unnerving, but in negotiations is handy: it's one way to deliver messages. He knew we were serious about starting quickly and he knew that I had White House support.

So we agreed to meet in Rome on April 24, and we went about preparing with the small team of people who had already come together—Gary Samore, George Look, and Ted Warner from the Office of the Secretary of Defense (OSD). We had good support from the entire interagency, but this small band at the outset was the one devoted full-time to the START follow-on negotiations. We sketched some initial ideas to offer up for the basic structure and substance of the agreement, with the goal of having a treaty framework ready by the time Presidents Obama and Medvedev would meet in Moscow in July. These ideas built on the statement by the presidents made in London on April 1: the negotiations would be about reducing and limiting strategic offensive arms, dropping to numbers lower than those achieved through the Moscow and START Treaties, and aiming for completion by the time that START went out of force in December 2009.

The Rome team was made up of George Look, Ted Warner, and me. We had hoped to have our JCS representative, Mike Elliott, on board in time to join us, but he was still transitioning from the U.S. Strategic Command in Omaha and could not make it. His first day on the job in the Pentagon was the very day we landed in Rome.

I have to admit I was nervous preparing for the meeting because it was my first official encounter with the Russians in my new capacity. I wanted to make sure that they understood that I had transitioned from my old nongovernmental role as the director of the Carnegie Moscow Center to become the U.S. government's official arms control negotiator. They had to understand that I was now invested with the authority of the president to get the job done. This notion is not always easy for the Russians and indeed for other foreigners because they do not have a system where political appointees come and go with each new government.

I was so nervous that I left my shirts behind, and upon unpacking in Rome found that I had my business suit but nothing to wear with it. I had only the cotton t-shirt I'd worn on the plane, which was not going to look good with the suit, either at the table or in our press encounter afterwards. So that evening, I went out on the swanky Via Veneto near the U.S. Embassy to see what I could find. Several smart boutiques seemed to have clothing only in the range of U.S. sizes 0–2, nothing larger. Although I don't consider myself large, I am not a size 2. Finally, some sympathetic ladies "of a certain age" (as the French would say) rooted around in the back room and came up with a silk shirt I could wear. I was ready to go into action.

FIRST ENCOUNTER WITH THE RUSSIANS

We met on April 24 in the U.S. Embassy in Rome, situated in an historic palace, the Palazzo Margherita. The embassy maintains its former grandeur in a few large spaces, including the ambassador's office. The working spaces are another matter—crammed full of office furniture, computers, and communications infrastructure, a bit scruffy overall. The palace was not optimized for modern office space, but it provided a glorious venue for our first meeting: the Red Ballroom.

The Red Ballroom seemed to me about the length of a U.S. football field. It had shiny parquet underfoot, its walls were covered with mirrors and red damask, and from the ceiling hung crystal chandeliers and red draperies. A long table was set up in the front right corner by the windows, and that is where we sat. We were dwarfed in the gigantic room. Antonov had two of his staff from the Ministry of Foreign Affairs with him and one Ministry of Defense (MOD) representative, but no one from the larger interagency in Moscow. In addition to George Look and Ted Warner, I had two notetakers from the embassy staff.

After some niceties, I launched into presenting our basic ideas for preparing a document in time for the presidents' meeting in July. Antonov did not let me get very far before interrupting, raising the proposal that the Bush administration had put on the table the previous October. Indeed, he said, the last time he had met with an American lady negotiator was to receive that very proposal from Paula DeSutter, my predecessor, who had also met with him in Rome. You already know our position on the new treaty, he said, because of the response that we gave to that proposal in December. Furthermore, he insisted, there should be a link to missile defense in the new treaty; the offense-defense relationship had to be addressed.

I answered him saying that we had more current instructions from the highest level: the London statement on the follow-on to START that had just been agreed by our presidents on April 1. I also reminded him that two statements had come out of the presidents' meeting in London: the first on the follow-on to START and the second on broad security cooperation. In that broader statement, I said, the presidents had been clear that the two sides should foster missile defense cooperation. The statement about the follow-on to START, however, had focused on achieving a treaty that would be about further strategic offensive reductions, not about missile defense. We needed to focus like a laser, I stressed, on getting that treaty finished. Cooperation on missile defense would be handled in another setting.

Over time, I have thought several things about Antonov's interruption. First, he may have needed to show his team that he could take the lead, knock me off balance, and steer the proceedings, even though the U.S. side was hosting. Second, he probably was trying to determine whether any aspect of the previous administration's proposal was still on the table. And third, perhaps he was used to more introductory niceties, more opportunities to exchange formalities and size each other up. The notion of an informal "nose touch," where we would get together and quickly exchange some early ideas, was not part of his lexicon. Perhaps, in this way, he mistook the meeting for a more formal plenary negotiating session. But that is my most charitable interpretation.

Luckily, I had excellent backup in both George Look and Ted Warner, who jumped in to reemphasize the points I was making and ensure that the Russian side took away the clear message that the Americans were all pulling in the same direction. If the Russians were expecting to see some differences at the table, there were none. Ted first showed his enormous skill at wearing the Russians down with abundant and unrelenting technical detail. Look conveyed the urgency with which the White House was treating this issue as well as the keen attention of President Obama.

We did not come away from the Red Ballroom with any idea about the substance that the Russians thought should go into the treaty. We did know what they didn't like because their December response to the Bush proposal had been critical. Antonov noted some nuanced changes from the previous approach in what we were proposing, but he did not offer up any ideas of his own. He did ask what reductions we were shooting for. Here Ted Warner had to convey that the level of reductions we were seeking was still under review, but he was certain we would have a proposal before the presidents met in July.

Despite the lack of substance, we did come away with a detailed and fast-paced work program, with meetings the first week of May in Washington, DC, the third week of May in Moscow, and the first week of June in Geneva, on the margins of the already-scheduled meeting of the Joint Compliance and Inspection Commission (JCIC), START's implementing body. To me, this was the most important message of the meeting—that we had the same sense of urgency and were working according to the same schedule, to be ready for a July summit.

I think there are some good reasons why the Russians had not done much thinking beyond their encounters with the Bush administration at the end of 2008. Antonov had not yet fully engaged the Russian interagency, and so he probably did not have a complete picture of how the Ministry of Defense and intelligence agencies would be playing in the negotiations. He also was seeing a new president, Medvedev, in action for the first time on his issues, and was perhaps not quite sure the role President Medvedev would play in relation to the prime minister, Vladimir Putin. In other words, he was not yet sure where his high-level marching orders would come from.

When the meeting adjourned, Antonov and I did a brief media event where we gave signals that the talks were off to a good start, but not much else. We didn't have anything to say, so the press went off into wider ranging questions on the Prague Initiative, conventional arms control in Europe, and a then-upcoming Non-Proliferation Treaty meeting. Photos of the two of us showed a fair level of comfort and accord. (See figure 3.) The negotiations were underway.

Chapter 4

The Run to Moscow

Treaty Lite or Full Caloric Content?

"They directed their negotiators to report on progress achieved in working out the new agreement by July 2009." These words ended the London joint statement, and it quickly followed that President Medvedev invited President Obama to come to Moscow. We were thus on a rapid-fire run to Moscow after the nose touch in Rome. We wanted to agree on a framework for the new treaty by that time and, if possible, on some new limits on delivery vehicles and warheads. New lower numbers would make the presidents' first full-scale summit productive and newsworthy, which both were clearly keen to achieve.

After an initial meeting in Washington, DC, the first week of May, Antonov and I agreed to bring the delegations together in Moscow in the third week of May, and again in the third week of June, within a few short weeks of the summit meeting. In between, we spent a good part of June in plenary meetings in Geneva, figuring out what the main elements of treaty structure and substance would be. The pace was intense, and it was unclear that we shared the same ideas about how the treaty should look.

The Russians were urging a "treaty-lite" on the model of the two-page 2002 Moscow Treaty, which was ironic, given that they had argued to the Bush team that they needed a new treaty more like START and less like SORT. By contrast, we wanted more written down, based on the model of START, which weighs in at over 600 pages. We were far apart on even this most basic point. I kept underscoring that we needed to go in search of a hybrid of START and SORT—the predictability that START's detailed verification regime provided, combined with the flexibility that was the overarching philosophy of SORT.

During the preparations for these meetings, the U.S. interagency team focused on the limits that we would be willing to accept for the new treaty. Since the Joint Chiefs of Staff had already done a considerable amount of analysis, we were willing to go lower than the final New START numbers in some cases. It was not a hard negotiation within the U.S. government, but we figured it would be a tougher one with the Russians.

The rest of the work we undertook was to ensure we knew what we wanted to preserve in terms of treaty structure. We knew we wanted to ensure that we could determine for ourselves the composition and structure of our strategic offensive forces—a concept that is known as "freedom to mix." Each party is allowed to choose how many warheads it wants to deploy at sea, how many on land, and how many on bombers, so long as these numbers stay within the limits of the treaty.

This concept has long been important in nuclear arms control because Russia and the United States are such different geopolitical actors. Russia is a great land power and has always had most of its armed forces deployed on land; it has struggled to gain access to the sea. The United States, by contrast, with direct access to two large oceans, has always been a sea-faring nation with a significant portion of its nuclear force structure in the Navy. The facts of geography being unchangeable, freedom to mix allows each country to build a nuclear force structure to suit its preferences—Russia more ICBMs, the United States more SLBMs, neither side deriving greater benefit from that fact.

We also knew we wanted to ensure that the technical core of START was sustained: clear definitions, informative notifications, well-structured data exchanges and, most importantly, effective verification, including on-site inspections. And we knew that we wanted to continue to protect our nuclear-armed allies, the United Kingdom and France, from being pulled into our bilateral negotiation—a demand that the Russians had been making, and Soviet negotiators before them, for decades.

Finally, we knew that we wanted some "good housekeeping" measures, such as the establishment of a body that would be able to resolve disputes during implementation of the treaty. Experience had taught us that such bodies could be valuable in solving technical problems, although they sometimes got bogged down, especially when the political environment between Moscow and Washington deteriorated. Even with the reset and better cooperation underway, we were not going to risk proceeding without a problem-solving mechanism.

We knew from Rome that the Russians were going to want some language on the offense-defense relationship in the treaty. I believed that as long as such language simply stated the relationship as a fact and did not commit us to any limits, we should be able to accept it. As an added insurance policy, I suggested to my colleagues that such language could be lodged in the preamble, which normally contains all kinds of hortatory statements but is not part of the legal obligations of the treaty. After some discussion, the interagency team agreed that we could try such an approach.

The initial meetings in Moscow were built around our first official plenaries, where each side gets to lay out its formal position and answer initial questions. On this occasion, Antonov did muster a full interagency delegation, which we were pleased to see because we had not been certain how the Ministry of Defense or the intelligence agencies, the Federal Security Bureau (FSB) and Main Directorate of the General Staff of the Armed Forces (GRU), would play. There were some familiar faces from the negotiations in the 1990s, such as Admiral Valentin Kuznetsov, who had been key to working definitions for the START Treaty. There were other familiar military faces, including Colonel Sergei Ryzhkov, who was a senior leader in the Russian Nuclear Risk Reduction Center (NRRC), the communication center for sending treaty notifications, and Colonel Yevgeny Il'in, who represented the MOD at the JCIC. We also saw some familiar faces who were well-known experts on missile technology, with links to the missile industry. Most importantly, the Russians brought two general officers to the table, General Sergei Orlov and General Viktor Poznihir, both of whom played important roles in the negotiations on critical issues such as telemetry. The signal was clear: the Russian government was taking this negotiation seriously.

That first Moscow meeting showed that we were far apart on the limitation numbers, with the Russian side wanting to maintain higher numbers of warheads while the U.S. side kept up numbers for delivery vehicles. In that early period, the Russians were not even clear that they would allow a limit on delivery vehicles, arguing that we should use "launchers" as the unit of account. We knew we had a hard slog ahead of us to agree on the central limits of the new treaty.

There was pressure to agree to them early, however, because the two presidents wanted it to be clear that they had engaged a negotiation that was moving forward quickly with the goals they had laid out in London —they wanted a "win" for their first summit meeting. Here too, it was necessary to engage in some hard bargaining, which would ultimately pull in the presidents themselves.

OPENING ROUND IN GENEVA

Once we had laid out our basic points in Moscow in May, we moved immediately to Geneva to continue hammering out a joint statement for July. It needed to be clear about the general concept and contours of the treaty, but it was not going to have much detail—unless we could agree quickly to the central limits.

Why Geneva? Normal negotiating practice would have had us moving to the other capital, to Washington, to conduct the next round—a practice not unlike ensuring two sports teams have equal "hometown advantage." Here Antonov argued that we needed to take advantage of the fact that the Russian delegation already had a long-planned JCIC meeting in Geneva in June, so additional experts would not be available to go to Washington.

For the longer run, both sides knew that switching back and forth across the ocean would be time-consuming and expensive, especially with so little time to prepare the treaty. We could depend on our long-established negotiating environment in Geneva—the U.S. and Russian Missions are close to each other, and both are practiced at supporting large delegations in a professional way. Moreover, Geneva is neutral territory convenient to both parties, the Swiss government ready to give rapid visa support to the Russians, which was also an important factor.

So I returned to the Brutalist building on the Route du Pregny where I had worked for the first time as a young State Department representative to the START talks in 1990. The building wasn't any more attractive, but an enterprising ambassador had tried his best to beautify the main entrance with a fountain and elaborate flower bed. It was a welcome addition.

The third floor was exactly as I remembered it, with large offices along a corridor, one assigned to each agency; sometimes as many as eight experts were crammed into each space. The secure facility or "SCIF" was still the same, cramped and hot; once inside, we were sealed in to ensure that no sounds could escape it. Instead of being stationed at a desk in one of the common spaces, however, this time my office was at the end of the hall—the chief negotiator's office. That was a big change from 1990, and it made me think about Richard Burt and Linton Brooks, the bosses I had worked for at that time. I hoped I could live up to their standards.

The meeting rooms were on the ground floor and had changed in the past twenty years. The big original hall for plenary meetings had been turned into a conference space for the U.S. Mission as a whole, so we could not count on it very often. Instead, we used a plenary meeting room that was a bit cramped, but it made passing notes among the delegation easier. The other meeting rooms on that floor came into heavy use once the individual working groups got underway. There was constant competition for meeting space with the rest of the U.S. Mission, so it was good that no other major negotiations were going on. I eventually apologized to the U.S. Mission and ambassador for being the New START "elephant," taking up a lot of space, heavy-footed and demanding.

The Russian Mission just down the street had not changed at all in thirty years. It was the same 1980s edifice, built in the final glory days of Soviet embassy architecture. (See figure 4.) Large chandeliers and massive artwork, including mosaics of Soviet scenes, were the order of the day, along with lots of marble. One important difference: The Soviet START negotiators had always sat the U.S. team on the side of the table facing the windows. During morning meetings, the U.S. chief negotiator had had the sun in his eyes, a normal Soviet practice to make the counterpart delegation uncomfortable. The first time I sat with the sun in my eyes, Antonov rather solicitously asked someone to pull the heavy drapes. That is when I thought that these negotiations might be different from START.

Sustaining that hopeful thought was complicated by resistance from my own team. Several of the very capable hands on my delegation had in mind those very START negotiations, which took about six years, on and off, to complete. They started out by insisting that we needed to follow established practice to communicate with the Russian delegation: send a fax requesting a meeting, wait for a reply, send a fax back confirming the meeting arrangements, wait for a fax back to say yes. Why not just pick up the phone and call them? I asked. Oh no, was the reply, the Russians may start to play games with that. Before you know it, you'll end up with them not showing up for meetings, or sending inappropriate people, claiming it's all our fault. In other words, from their START experience, we needed a thorough paper trail to organize a meeting.

With such procedures, however, we were never going to get the new treaty finished in six months. We did not have that kind of time. Let's just try calling them, I said, and see how it goes. If they start to play games, then we will fix it. OK, was the reply, but you know that they don't answer their office phones for two hours at lunchtime and after 6:00 pm in the evening. In that case, I said, you'd better get their mobile phone numbers and give them yours, so you can communicate any time of the day or night as needed. If you need a paper trail, I said, you can send them a text message.

That idea really raised eyebrows, and some of my most experienced hands decided that they did not want to return for the later negotiating rounds. Although I was sorry to see them go, the delegation did need to accommodate new communication technology, if only to establish the pace that we would have to keep up for the coming months. I will say that I really appreciated what the old hands had taught me about proper recordkeeping, which is all-important in ensuring that both we and the Russians were operating off the same texts, in English and Russian, at every moment. This is especially important when negotiations are moving rapidly, and many changes are being introduced every day.

Technology has also had an odd and negative effect on recordkeeping, which many archivists and historians mourn. In the old days, the negotiating record of a treaty was kept in paper copies piling up in vaults and libraries, including the written journals that were sometimes kept by chief negotiators and members of their teams. These were and continue to be a gold mine for historians. Nowadays, many negotiating exchanges take place in texts or messaging applications such as WhatsApp. These are more difficult to save and record for history; sometimes they are even designed to delete automatically in a short period.

Of course, there have always been ephemera in negotiations—the ideas jotted down on paper napkins during a meal, the conversation at a reception that later blooms into a new proposal. Unless someone is a committed diarist, such actions are lost to history. However, I would say that the current texting phenomenon, while it has sped up negotiations considerably, also comes at a cost to our understanding of a treaty's genesis.

I, for one, am sorry that I could not figure out a way to keep the text where I told my counterpart, Anatoly Antonov, that we needed to have a new "walk in the woods." I was referring to the July 1982 walk that every arms control student knows about, when Paul Nitze took a walk with his Soviet counterpart, Yuli Kvitsinsky, to break a logjam in the Intermediate-Range Nuclear Forces (INF) negotiations. Still racing to get the treaty done by December, we needed to break through an important logjam in November 2009. Like our predecessors, we walked and talked, not in the woods, but through the neighborhoods behind the Russian and U.S. Missions. Like our predecessors, we did not successfully break the logjam, but we did develop a new sense that we were in this together, that we would succeed or crash and burn jointly.

Many negotiators, on both sides of the table, have come to this realization before us. Their memoirs recount that mutual trust and a sense of urgency are key factors in getting through a difficult negotiation, along with a mutual willingness to take risks and be creative. Often such risk-taking creativity gets slapped down, for the capitals do not appreciate it. But sometimes, it pays dividends.

DELEGATIONS SETTLE IN

With the departures at the end of the first round, I quickly lost my executive secretariat, which could have spelled disaster for keeping on top of both the paper trail and the meeting planning. Luckily, I had Karen Kirchgasser. I had first met Karen in Moscow while I was director of the Carnegie Moscow Center. She was working for William Burns, the ambassador in Moscow, at the heart of his executive secretariat. During that time, she was diagnosed with breast cancer and had to curtail her time in Moscow, to her great disappointment, returning to Washington,

DC, early for treatment. When I took the New START job, Karen asked if she could join the delegation, and she had come out to Geneva as part of the State team working with Marcie Ries. It was Marcie who suggested that Karen would make a great executive secretary.

When I first approached Karen about it, she blanched, but she turned out to be a perfect fit for the job. Early on, she understood that she had to establish a professional relationship with Sergei Rudenko, the executive secretary on the Russian side. Each had to be comfortable calling the other late at night or on weekends to schedule urgent meetings. They were both pivotal in making complex arrangements for two high-level meetings between General Nikolai Makarov, the Russian chief of the General Staff, and Admiral Michael Mullen, the chairman of the Joint Chiefs of Staff, and for quickly making arrangements for presidential meetings, including in Copenhagen in December, and for the signing ceremony in Prague in April. They continued to use fax machines when they needed to, but mostly they used their mobile phones.

Karen relished the title the Russians used for her, "IspolSek," Implementation Secretary; she said it made her feel like a big deal. Sadly, her cancer returned once we were finished in Geneva and the treaty had been ratified and entered into force. She died in 2012, and her many friends and colleagues mourned her passing. There is a fitting tribute to her at the National Zoo in Washington, DC. If you take a walk to the carousel, sit and watch the action from the bench that is dedicated to her. It is a good place to contemplate the merry-go-round of diplomatic work, which sometimes spins off a success. Karen Kirchgasser made a big contribution to the success of the New START Treaty.

I do not know the details, but I know that Anatoly Antonov had his share of troubles getting the Russian delegation up and running. Moscow had to be "all in" to ensure that he could order essential office supplies and that he had adequate typists and support personnel for the cable system. In 2009, the Russian Ministry of Foreign Affairs was not allowing official communications to be made via email, so every detail every day had to be reported in official cables. Having the right personnel available to pump out the cables—and not only those writing the reports—was a big deal. Because the Russian president himself had launched the negotiations as a high priority, Antonov evidently got the support he needed—but he told me he breathed a sigh of relief when the Xerox paper actually arrived.

The rhythm of reporting and the Moscow-Washington time difference affected the schedules of both delegations. The opening of business in Moscow is two hours earlier than the opening of business in Geneva, so the Russian delegation had to complete all reporting about the day's meetings on that same day. Sometimes they worked far into the night to ensure that all the cables got off in time. Antonov read every one of them, so sometimes he was at the Russian Mission until 1:00 or 2:00 in the morning. Afterwards, he told me, he would take a long night walk through the neighborhood to unwind, hoping Moscow wouldn't wake him up with questions at 7:00 a.m. They always had questions in the morning.

By contrast, because Washington's opening of business was six hours after ours in Geneva, the U.S. delegation operated in relative peace from 8:00 a.m. to 2:00 p.m., finishing up and sending cables from the day before, in addition to sending emails. We did supplement the cable reporting with frequent emails over the secure system, which allowed us to communicate with colleagues in the Washington agencies relatively quickly. Once 2:00 p.m. came around, though, we normally faced a barrage of questions and requests for information, and we were regularly sending questions and requests for guidance in Washington's direction as well. Our active day thus often went on until 9:00 or 10:00 at night.

This difference in "battle rhythm" on the two delegations did not have a real impact on the negotiations, I believe, although sometimes the fact that Washington had not yet woken up and provided new guidance was a source of hectoring by the Russian side. We generally took it in good humor, given how we could point out plenty of instances when the Russian delegation was waiting for instructions. Waiting for Godot, I called it.

FINAL PREPARATIONS FOR SUMMIT

We went back to Moscow in late June to continue hammering out the Joint Understanding. Like every negotiator before me, I wanted to hand the president a finished document when he arrived two weeks later. Like most negotiators before me, I could not get it done—it would take the presidents to reach final agreement. We were able to bring practically everything to a close, except the numbers for the central limits of the treaty.

Stress was already bearing down on the delegation. I was working in one part of the secure facility in the Moscow embassy when Mike Elliott ran in to tell me that Ted Warner was not well. He had simply stopped talking, hearing, or seeing for a few moments, completely freezing up. We immediately got Ted into an ambulance to a clinic. John Beyrle, the ambassador, and his staff were absolutely fantastic in getting things to move quickly.

This situation was terrifying, but it was not the first or the last time that we had stress-related medical incidents in the delegation. Teeth or hair falling out, high blood pressure, shingles—we did not suffer every stress-related disease in the book, but sometimes it seemed to me that we had.

Today reading through the July Joint Understanding, I have to laugh remembering some of the convoluted conversations that we had to put it together during that June in Geneva and Moscow. The first paragraph contains the phrase "*inter alia*" (Latin for "among others"), which resulted after Antonov and I argued at length over whether the document needed to indicate all the provisions of the new treaty—his view, or we could add some provisions, the necessity of which became clear in the course of the negotiations—my view. In the end, we agreed to include "*inter alia*," but only after consultation with the Russian lawyers to ensure that some American trap was not hidden in those two Latin words.

The exact limits had to wait for the endgame to the negotiations, but we also had to discuss at length whether we could indicate a range of numbers for delivery vehicles and warheads. I think that the Russians were uncomfortable to convey publicly what the differences were because everyone would assume that they preferred the higher end of the range. In the end, though, they agreed, but they also made the interesting suggestion that we should have provisions for calculating those limits—in other words, agreeing to the notion that we should not simply replicate the counting rules of the START Treaty.

Their clearest signal on treaty structure came in the paragraph where they emphasized that yes, the new treaty would need verification procedures and related measures, but "adapted, simplified and made less costly, as appropriate, in comparison to the START Treaty." They were signaling early on that they did not see the new treaty as being identical to START, and indeed, they were looking for efficiencies in the verification regime. Because U.S. weapon systems operators had a similar preference, we could agree to adopt this approach.

Wrapping up was a straightforward mention that the treaty would have a duration of ten years, unless superseded by another treaty. There was no mention at this phase of a five-year extension clause.

Notably, only a few short months after the April joint statement, reality had begun to sink in regarding how long it would take to negotiate the new treaty. In London, the presidents had stated that the two countries intended to conclude this agreement before the START Treaty would expire in December 2009. In the end, the Moscow statement said only that the presidents directed their negotiators to finish their work on the treaty at an early date. This formulation reflected Russian skepticism that the new treaty could be completed so quickly, although both delegations continued to drive hard to make it happen.

The summit statement was called "The Joint Understanding for the START Follow-On Treaty." At that time, the new treaty did not yet have a name, so it was called simply the "START Follow-On" in everything from the international media to cable reporting. U.S. cables are marked with numbers prefixed "SFO"; the name "New START" only emerged in the endgame.

Obama in Moscow

Obama's first summit meeting with the Russian president in Moscow is, I admit, a hazy memory for me, because I was so preoccupied with making sure that the Joint Understanding came together. Until the very last minute, we were dickering over how to treat the numbers. In the end, the Russians did agree to state them as a range: 500 to 1,100 delivery vehicles and 1,500 to 1,675 warheads.

I remember that this agreement was reached only after the two presidents discussed it at the last minute, and that made sense to me. The Joint Understanding is a highly useful document for negotiators, giving a good deal of instruction about the treaty structure and substance. It is not, however, an exciting document that would send the message to the world that the two presidents are serious about nuclear reductions. They wanted to make that message clear, and to do that, some indication had to be given that we were willing to go lower than the 2,200 warheads that were permitted under the Moscow Treaty of 2002.

The Joint Understanding did make a splash in the press, the biggest of the summit meeting. A press conference was called to discuss it, and I made myself available to answer any technical questions. Oddly, Dennis McDonough, deputy national security advisor for Strategic Communications, Gary Samore, the White House coordinator for arms control and WMDs, and Michael McFaul, the senior director for Russia, told me that my services were not needed, so I sat it out in the audience.

Clearly, the White House saw this as a presidential moment, and not a moment for the State Department to be in the picture.

Indeed, Secretary of State Clinton had recently broken her elbow and had decided not to travel to Moscow, so the State Department by natural coincidence was not much in the picture. Secretary Clinton's misfortune had a bright side for me, however. When I arrived at the Ritz where the president and the U.S. delegation were staying, I got a call from the U.S. protocol officer in charge of assigning rooms: I had a special room assigned to me, but I had to be out of it at exactly the time when the president would be leaving the hotel to depart Moscow. Not a moment more.

When I got to the room, I could see why: I had evidently been assigned the suite that had been reserved for Secretary Clinton. It was beautiful, with space for the large staff that normally accompanied her on all trips; I was rattling around in it. And I was much too anxious about the negotiations to enjoy it. I probably spent a total of six hours sleeping in the room, with all the tense negotiating sessions and late nights.

When the president's motorcade pulled away from the Ritz's front door, I was elsewhere in the hotel dealing with some loose ends. My mobile phone rang, and the protocol officer asked me why I was not out of the room yet. I raced upstairs, threw what remained to be packed in my bag, and left—maybe fifteen minutes after the president had departed. The cleaning crew was already waiting outside the room. The Ritz probably had an oligarch waiting to move in. I took off on foot to the other, cheaper hotel where my delegation was staying, for we had more work to do before we could leave Moscow.

Strolling the Kremlin

I chuckle when I think of the contrast on that occasion between me and those in the president's security "bubble." They moved strictly by motorcade and absolutely had to be in that motorcade, or they would not get to where the president was going. By contrast, I had a lapel pin and paperwork authorizing me to get into venues when I needed to, and so I could move from place to place if I was not in the president's meetings. I had just spent three years living in Moscow as the director of the Carnegie Moscow Center, so I knew the center of the city well. It was a bit like coming home: I even took an hour off to drop by the Carnegie offices on Pushkin Square to say hello to my old colleagues and staff.

My best adventure roaming around on that occasion was getting into the Kremlin for the reception and state dinner. I asked our security team if my official invitation and identification would be sufficient to walk in, and they assured me that they would. So after finishing some work, I walked up to the Borovitsky Gate, the main vehicle gate of the Kremlin, and presented my credentials. The guards were surprised to see me arriving on foot rather than in a BMW or Mercedes, but eventually they let me walk in to the beautiful banqueting rooms in the Grand Kremlin Palace.

There I found gathered the cream of the Moscow intellectual and political elite, drinking champagne, eating canapés, and waiting for the Americans to arrive. As often happens in such circumstances, the president was running late, and the rest of the Americans were with him in his motorcade. Moscow traffic did not help. For an hour, I wandered around the crowd, catching up with people whom I had not seen since leaving Carnegie, listening to the gossip, and trying as best I could to be the sole American representative. It was enjoyable, but I wish I had been able to take notes.

When the president finally arrived, we went straight into the state dinner, so the Russians must have been a bit miffed that they did not get access to the larger delegation. In any event, the banquet proceeded in good spirits, although at high speed because everyone in both official parties was tired. I do remember the food was wonderful, the best that Russian chefs have to offer, and wished we had had more time to savor it. Our plates, however, were whisked away quickly so that we could get through the six courses in an hour. The toasts were very warm and indicated that the two presidents were serious about improving U.S.-Russian relations—the famous "reset."

The Moscow Summit meeting set in motion the negotiations that would carry us forward to treaty completion. Having the presidents give us two instruction documents in short order—London in April and Moscow in July—gave both delegations the bureaucratic firepower we needed to get things done quickly. That included dealing with the different government agencies and even the mundane arrangements. I was able to convince the U.S. Mission in Geneva that we really did need two full floors of office space, for example, and Antonov was finally getting all the Xerox paper and secretarial support he needed. Now we just had to nail down the treaty structure and begin to negotiate treaty language.

CHAPTER 5

OCTOBER BREAKTHROUGH ON VERIFICATION

VITAL AGREEMENT, VITAL DIFFERENCES

From our earliest plenaries in Geneva in August and September 2009, the Russians made clear that the new treaty would have to differ from the old in one important aspect: mobile ground-based missiles had to be treated the same as mobile sea- and air-based systems. In other words, their mobile ICBM force was no different as a verification problem than the U.S. SLBM force or the bombers. This was a significant change from START, which was negotiated when both countries thought they would be deploying mobile ICBMs—as it turned out, only the Russians did. The Russians argued that they were bearing a greater burden during inspections than the United States, which ran against the principle of reciprocity in treaty practice. Therefore, they wanted some streamlining.

That streamlining translated into fewer inspections—the number that the Russians first put on the table was twelve in contrast to twenty-eight under START. They also introduced the notion of seven additional "visits" to check on systems that were not deployed—in storage, for example, or which had been converted to other missions or eliminated. These visits were to be less demanding than inspections, with fewer negotiated rules. The Russians had the idea that the negotiations should start with a blank page for the verification regime, not taking advantage of the experience gained in START, and keeping the language vague.

The U.S. team, by contrast, was intent on updating START. After fifteen years of START inspections, the interagency had come to the conclusion that some of the START inspections could be combined, consolidated, or eliminated so as to make New START inspections simpler, less costly, and less of a burden on nuclear base operations.

We also wanted some things fixed. Under START, the Russians had begun the practice of flushing mobile ICBMs when they knew an inspection was underway, using the time from initial notification to the arrival of the inspectors at the deployment base to get as many missiles as possible into the field, where inspectors would not have access to them. That had led to some sharp exchanges during START implementation meetings.

Most importantly, early on we concluded that we could improve knowledge of real deployments if we could dispense with the counting rules that had dominated earlier arms control treaties, including START. The counting rule for ICBMs, for example, designated each missile of a class to have a certain number of warheads, determined by the maximum number that had been observed in flight testing. In that way, the Soviet SS-18 heavy missile was determined to have ten warheads, although its carrying capacity is much greater—reckoned by some to be fourteen or even more.

This approach had come to penalize the U.S. SLBMs, which according to the START counting rule could carry eight warheads each. In fact, the United States had decided to begin downloading the SLBM force, so actual warhead deployments on each missile were fewer than eight. As a result, the START database showed higher numbers of U.S. SLBM warheads than what actually existed on the missiles. We wanted to fix that problem.

We were keen to fix other lingering problems from START as well, especially the "phantom" bombers that the Russians kept insisting should remain under accounting even though we had converted them to non-nuclear delivery vehicles or eliminated them. Both B-52 and B-1 bombers were caught in this problem, although with differences: the B-1s had all been converted to conventional armaments only. By contrast, older B-52s had been completely eliminated. They sit in a bomber boneyard at Davis-Monthan Air Force Base in Arizona.

We also needed to ensure that the verification measures were tailored to the limits of the new treaty and did not simply replicate START in a way that had no purpose for this treaty. Here was where the great telemetry debate began. The sharing of telemetry data, essentially flight test data for missiles, had an important function under START because it was used to confirm the viability of the counting rules: a missile was considered to carry the maximum number of reentry vehicles for warheads with which it had been tested. The way each side confirmed that maximum number was to exchange telemetry about flight tests under detailed START procedures.

In New START, since we discarded the counting rules in favor of counting declared warheads on the front of missiles, we did not need telemetry measures in the new treaty. However, telemetry became an important confidence-building aspect of the negotiations, and it came to be important in the ratification debate in the Senate.

So both the U.S. and Russian sides entered the negotiations with some improvements that we wanted to see made to the verification regime in the new treaty. Everyone understood how the START verification regime worked, but each side had different reasons to try to overhaul it. The Russians wanted more of a minimalist approach, and the U.S. side wanted some streamlining too. Each side had a hard job convincing the other about what fixes were needed, but the process in the end led to some important innovations that opened the door to treaties of the future.

The initial struggle with the Russians was over their "blank-page" approach, not wanting to take advantage of the knowledge gained from START implementation and looking for vaguer procedures. The United States wanted START updated but not discarded, and we understood the clear necessity of describing the procedures in some detail.

Once again, the situation was ironic because the Russians had argued mightily with the Bush administration that they wanted to maintain START verification procedures in a new treaty. The Bush team, in turn, had pressed for the blank page—or indeed, no verification measures at all. Strange as it may seem, this phenomenon occurs often in strategic arms negotiations. Ed Ifft, a seasoned negotiator who was the senior State Department representative on the START delegation, coined a rule to describe it: the two sides have the same positions, but never at the same time.

To safeguard U.S. interests, the U.S. team under the leadership of Ted Warner took the initiative to develop a new verification concept. The process began in September 2009, when it became clear the Russians were gunning to adjust the approach to mobile missile verification. We needed to ensure that we knew what was going on with the Russian ICBM force. At the same time, and as always, we wanted to limit Russian access to what they really needed to know about *our* ICBM force. Both sides wanted to ensure that we were not imposing costs on our operational commanders by interfering too much, through the inspection process, at their bases. Too frequent or overly intrusive inspections could disrupt operational tempo for days, and both sides wanted to avoid that.

Ted had already brought together a small brain trust of experts that became known as the Inspection Protocol Working Group. These people understood the START verification regime as well as the issues that had been raised by both sides. State, Defense, JCS, Energy and the intelligence community were all well-represented. The level of expertise was exceptional and included those who were weapon systems operators and so had been on the receiving side of inspections, as well as those who were experienced inspectors. I thought it was the ideal mix of people to come up with an innovative verification regime for the new treaty.

Ted instructed his team in September to boil down what we needed to its essence. They began by scrubbing through the START verification regime, determining what was really needed to monitor deployed and non-deployed nuclear weapon systems. We already understood that the new treaty would substitute the counting rule approach with counting warheads, but how would inspections to confirm declared warhead numbers fit with other inspections? The team also thought long and hard about what was actually needed to monitor the mobile missiles in the Russian ICBM force.

When we came back to the plenary meeting table in late September, the Russians were still intent on inspections for deployed missile systems and warheads as well as visits with vague procedures to account for non-deployed systems. They were also sticking to their low number of annual inspections.

That round of late September plenaries was difficult. It got us to the point of agreeing on the structure of the treaty regime—a three-tiered approach with a treaty text, a protocol to cover more detailed issues, and annexes to describe procedures. All three parts would be an inherent part of the whole, and all would be legally binding. However, we were still struggling with the Russian insistence on starting with a "blank page" and did not get to a big breakthrough on the verification regime. We all realized that the clock was ticking. We needed to accelerate the talks, or we would never have the treaty ready by December 5, in time to replace START.

THE STUDY BREAK

Ted came to me at the end of the round, when both delegations were preparing to go back to their respective capitals for a few weeks to work out further instructions. Rather than having everyone in our delegation return to Washington, DC, Ted told me that it made more sense to leave a small team behind in Geneva, where they could concentrate on developing a verification concept to carry the talks forward quickly. The concept could then be presented to the Washington interagency. If Washington was sold on it, then it could be presented in a coherent way to the Russians when we got back together in Geneva in October.

This study break in Geneva produced a dramatic new concept for verification. It consolidated twelve different types of START inspections into two major types of inspections, for deployed systems, which would be Type 1 inspections, and non-deployed systems, which would be Type 2 inspections. In Type 1 inspections, several activities would be carried out, including confirming the number of warheads declared on reentry vehicles and ensuring that the data we had about the presence of Russian missiles at bases were accurate. Essentially, the focus of Type 1 inspections would be on operating bases and the weapon systems present there, and these inspections would be used to confirm several aspects of their status —numbers of missiles, numbers of warheads, and deployment locations. Type 2 inspections, by contrast, would focus on non-operational bases; that is, storage and maintenance facilities, or facilities where systems were being converted or eliminated.

The beauty of this concept was that it retained all of the tasks present in the twelve types of START inspection but folded them into only two. For example, START data update inspections, formerly declared facility inspections, along with conversion or elimination inspections, were all folded into Type 2 inspections. The inspections would take place over a longer period to accommodate the multiple tasks, but individual facilities would not be inspected as frequently, and their operations would not be interrupted as often.

Some of the ideas that the brain trust devised ended up being important endgame issues for the negotiations. For example, they determined that if each launcher and delivery vehicle had a unique identifying number, which would be recorded in the database and tracked through constant notifications, then we would be in an improved position to monitor the Russian ICBM force on a 24/7 basis. Importantly, inspectors would have a clearer picture of what missiles should be present when they arrived at an operating base.

Understanding that, the Russians threw up all kinds of objections, even to the point of claiming that inscribing unique identifying numbers on the sides of their missiles would interfere with missile flight. Finally, after exchanges on the matter between Admiral Mullen and General Makarov, the most senior military commanders, and even between President Obama and President Medvedev, the two sides agreed that the existing serial numbers that each side used to track and account for their weapon systems would be used for this purpose. A simple solution, but one that has proven vital to the effectiveness of New START verification.

The lesson that I learned from this experience is a lesson that would serve well, I believe, in any negotiation: sometimes it pays dividends to turn loose the experts and let them think through, over, and around a problem until they come up with a solution that works for all. We were lucky to have an experienced team lead, Ted Warner, who knew a great deal about past arms control regimes but was not so wedded to the old ways that he would not consider how to adjust them to new circumstances. I also think the dynamics among the U.S. experts were important: the weapon systems operators knew the operational costs that inspections could impose, and the inspectors knew what they needed to verify that treaty commitments were being respected. The "creative combat" that ensued between them ensured that the United States got exactly what it needed from New START: effective verification at a reasonable cost to U.S. operational tempo.

WARHEAD COUNTING

Beyond the verification concept, the most important innovation in the treaty was dispensing with the counting rules for ICBMs and SLBMs.

The bombers were another matter, which I will address separately. We thought long and hard about how to confirm the number of warheads that we or the Russians would declare on an individual missile. The basic breakthrough was the ability to physically check and count what was on the front end of each type of missile, which we accomplished through reentry vehicle on-site inspection. Inspectors would be given the opportunity to count objects on the front ends of missiles, which would be opened but covered with a soft or pliable cover so that objects could be counted.

One problem was that every object on the front end of a missile is not a nuclear warhead. Both sides deploy penetration aids, chaff dispensers, or decoys that are used to spoof missile defenses. They are conventional, not nuclear, objects. To differentiate between them, we came up with the idea that inspectors would be able to use detection devices to determine that an object was non-nuclear in nature. In other words, inspectors would be able to confirm the number of nuclear objects declared; if there were extras, they would be able to determine that these were not nuclear warheads.

It sounds easy but required some complex and difficult discussions. For example, how pliable should the soft cover be that is used during the inspections? There could be no question that a warhead was hiding under a cover that did not properly display the number of objects underneath. What kind of radiation detector could be used? Both sides were resolved that the detection equipment should be able to determine that an object is non-nuclear but not discover any design secrets in the adjacent warheads. Many technical discussions ensued, leading to detailed procedures so that each side could check and accept the other's detection equipment.

Another aspect of these inspections that was complicated to determine is how the missile to be inspected is selected. Clearly, neither the United States nor Russia would want inspectors to have access to every single missile in a unit. Such extensive access would prolong an inspection to such a point that base operations would be seriously impeded. Foreign inspectors on site for so long would also potentially endanger secrets that each side wants to keep. In the end, we went with usual inspection practice, wherein the inspecting party gets to select at random the missile to be inspected.

Reentry vehicle on-site inspection has now been extensively tested in practice in New START, and it has allowed us to solve our dilemma of counting warheads on SLBMs. It has also opened the door to the possibility of warhead inspections in the future. Earlier arms control treaties had focused on counting delivery vehicles and launch systems— missiles, submarines, bombers—because they were large objects that could be easily counted, even from outer space. Warheads were constrained by dint of their association with their delivery vehicles—the counting rules. Once the delivery vehicles were eliminated, the warheads went into storage and were no longer considered a threat.

Such an approach also meant that we could not, or did not try to, distinguish conventional from nuclear missiles. Getting direct access to the missiles to determine if they were nuclear or conventional was considered too sensitive. For that reason, the 1987 Short- and Intermediate-Range Nuclear Forces Treaty (INF), although it has nuclear in its name, banned all ground-launched missiles between 500 and 5,500 km in range— conventional *and* nuclear. Moving away from the counting rule and focusing on confirming what is actually on the front end of missiles was a big change from the past, but it also opened up new opportunities for future arms control agreements. In particular, banning or limiting nuclear warheads while letting conventionally armed missiles continue to be deployed becomes an option.

Thus the New START verification regime has a bigger value than the treaty itself: it bodes well for future arms control regimes that focus more on accounting for warheads, nuclear or conventional, than has been possible in the past. In the end, I believe both we and the Russians got what we wanted: streamlined inspection procedures at a sufficient level of detail to be effectively implemented. We made good use of what had been used in previous treaties, but we were not trapped into perpetrating problems, such as overcounting of warheads, that were not in our interest. Most importantly, we did not end up with a blank page or vague language but rather with detailed procedures that make the inspections reliable in confirming information that the Russians provide us. The same, of course, goes for them.

CHAPTER 6

Senate Observer Group in Geneva

Senate Advice and Consent

Since nuclear arms control talks began, the U.S. executive branch has had a hard time keeping the legislative branch away from the negotiating table. There is a good reason for that. In constitutional terms, it is the president's prerogative to conduct foreign policy; if he negotiates a treaty, he does so with an executive branch team. However, he must bring it to the Senate for advice and consent before he can ratify and bring it into force. The Congress also holds the purse strings, controlling the budget for foreign policy initiatives and national security alike—the defense budget being of particular importance. So, despite the president's constitutional role, the legislative branch has powerful tools to steer and influence the president's policy, and sometimes to veto it.

Congress' interest in arms control has ranged over time from profound suspicion (will this president give up too much?) to a desire to influence the process in a certain direction, to a positive urge to prepare for the ratification debate. But from the president's perspective, even the best objectives grounded in goodwill could not justify giving legislators a regular seat at the negotiating table. It would undermine his authority under the Constitution. Long ago, therefore, some way had to be found to address this conundrum.

The Senate Arms Control Observer Group first took shape during 1985, when the United States was negotiating with the Soviet Union on the Intermediate-Range Nuclear Forces Treaty (INF) and while the first Strategic Arms Reduction Treaty (START) talks were also in the offing. It was created to be bipartisan, allowing senators to join arms control negotiations periodically as observers. The official purpose of the group was to advise U.S. arms control negotiating teams, and to "monitor and report to the Senate on the progress and development of negotiations." As Senator Sam Nunn, one of the original members, said at the time, "The goal was to have the Senate fulfill both halves of its constitutional responsibilities, not only the consent half—that's we've been looking to primarily in the past—but also the advice half."[1]

In 1999, the role of the group expanded to consider a wider set of issues such as missile defense and to participate in talks related to them. Its name was then changed to the National Security Working Group with the same general goal of nurturing a bipartisan group of senators who were knowledgeable about the issues and at least somewhat invested in them. During the next decade, however, the group rarely met, and the level of interest in arms control and related national security issues fell sharply in the Senate.

It was only after President Obama and President Medvedev signed their July 2009 statement in Moscow that interest in the working group began to revive. Inside the administration, we recognized that the level of knowledge and interest in the Senate about arms control matters had dropped off in the two decades since the Cold War. If senators could not or would not engage the administration on the new treaty, it was unlikely to be ratified. Thus, we saw the working group as a good way to work early and often with the Senate. We briefed the group many times on the road to ratification.

Senator Lugar encouraged us. A prominent Republican with long-standing bipartisan credentials on nuclear policy, he would be the "trail boss" on the Republican side of the aisle for taking the treaty through the advice-and-consent process in the Senate. Highly supportive of the negotiations, from the very outset he was firm in his belief that there would be enough Republican votes to get the treaty across the finish line, if it were properly negotiated in line with U.S. national security interests. He stressed, however, that the level of knowledge and understanding of nuclear weapons and arms control policy had fallen off, and he urged us to engage as much as possible.

Although the National Security Working Group never attracted a large group of senators during the New START talks, those who did participate were highly influential in the ratification process. On the Republican side, Senator Jon Kyl was the lead player and a tough interlocutor who knew what he wanted. He had become concerned about the state of the U.S. nuclear weapons stockpile and wanted to ensure that funding for fissile material facilities, including production of plutonium pits for warheads, was assured. He was also keen to see the U.S. proceed with modernization of its nuclear triad, which would involve funding for new submarines, bombers, and intercontinental ballistic missiles. For Senator Kyl, it was unjustified to pursue a new nuclear arms reduction treaty if those issues went untended.

On the Democratic side of the aisle, Senator John Kerry, chairman of the Senate Foreign Relations Committee, and Senator Carl Levin, chairman of the Armed Services Committee, were strong leaders who ensured that President Obama's priorities received attention, pushing back against unfair critiques or issues that were irrelevant. They were a steady presence on the National Security Working Group both before and after the New START Treaty came into force.

While the treaty was being negotiated in 2009, however, it was Senator Dianne Feinstein, chairman of the Senate Select Committee on Intelligence, who played the predominant role. Senator Feinstein was a good friend of my boss, Ellen Tauscher, who appealed to her after the July Moscow meeting to become actively engaged to rev up interest in the negotiations on both sides of the aisle, and to engage with Senator Kyl. Senator Feinstein was a highly effective partner.

THE THIRD DEGREE IN GENEVA

When we dove back into the talks in Geneva in August and September, it quickly became clear that we could expect a visitation from the National Security Working Group in the fall. I was enthusiastic because I saw the necessity of gaining greater Senate interest in and understanding of our work. I was also cautious because I knew the visit would have to be carefully managed, including with the Russians, who would be asked to engage with the group as well. The old timers in the delegation were gloomy, remembering the visits of the Arms Control Observer Group in the 1980s as efforts to meddle in the negotiations and sometimes to undermine them. I told my delegation that no matter what, we would welcome the team and make the best of their visit in every way we could.

The visit took longer to arrange than expected, and in the end only Senators Kyl and Feinstein were slated to arrive, each with one staffer. The date was set for November 10–13, which ended up being a crunch time for the negotiations. At the same time, we were arranging a meeting between Admiral Mullen, the chairman of the Joint Chiefs of Staff, and General Makarov, chief of the Russian General Staff, scheduled for November 23–24. Thanksgiving was coming, and people were eager to get home to celebrate with their families. The pressure from the White House for greater speed and more results was growing fast.

I was determined to make it work no matter what, but we had some stiff requests to deal with. With memories gone of what had happened in the 1980s, demands came down for the senators to sit at the negotiating table and participate in plenary meetings. We had to gently remind that the role of senators was to observe, not negotiate. Therefore, we would brief them thoroughly and repeatedly, including in classified settings, about the progress in the negotiations and make sure they had direct access and opportunity to talk with my counterpart on the Russian side, Anatoly Antonov and, with his guidance, to his delegation.

The negotiations concerning the access and activities of the working group were nearly as difficult as what we were going through in Geneva with the Russians, but Ellen Tauscher did much of the work. A former congresswoman from California, Tauscher was an expert on horse trading and a serious street fighter. The White House was also involved to ensure that there was no damage to the president's prerogative regarding the conduct of foreign policy.

When I approached Antonov about the upcoming visit, to my surprise he was very amenable. He suggested hosting a lunch for the senators during which they could talk with a number of those in his delegation and ask as many questions as they wanted. He also informed me that, of course, there would be a delegation arriving from the Russian State Duma and Federation Council, who would want to meet with me and my delegation. I was not surprised, but I was amused, and it proved to be a pattern: whenever I stated the need to engage the Senate to ensure a smooth ratification process, he insisted that he had the very same problem and that his legislators would have to be engaged too.

On the arrival day, I went to the airport twice, first to meet Senator Feinstein, who arrived with her husband, and later, Senator Kyl. I knew I was in trouble when Senator Kyl saw me waiting and, with a bright smile, asked me how I had time to be at the airport—should I not be at the negotiating table? I explained to him that we always took a break at midday so that the Russians could have their lunch: unlike Americans, they were not satisfied with sandwiches at their desks; they wanted a hot meal.

My ride with him and his staffer in the car to the hotel was useful because it was clear that he was there to work—he did not want to do anything in Geneva other than visit the delegations. We immediately scheduled our first meeting for the early evening.

Senator Feinstein too was ready to get down to business and had a particular issue on her mind: the status of some measures that had been a big part of the START Treaty, but which we were examining to see whether they really needed to be in the START follow-on. At the time, START had been in implementation since 1994 and had been a successful treaty. It had been the tool by which the nuclear weapon systems left in Ukraine, Kazakhstan, and Belarus at the breakup of the Soviet Union had been eliminated. Thus, Senator Feinstein and others on Capitol Hill wanted to know why we were thinking about any changes to the START regime at all.

When the senators arrived at the U.S. Mission in Geneva, we immediately went into the secure facility, the SCIF, with their staffers and my senior delegation members. We began briefing them on the progress of the various parts of the new treaty: Ted Warner took on the inspection regime, Mike Elliott conversions and eliminations, Dick Trout the database, and Kurt Siemon the notifications, definitions, and telemetry. The senators immediately latched on to telemetry as an urgent topic. They had heard that it was an issue up for grabs in the new treaty: why was that, given that it had been such an important part of START?

Telemetry data are the signals transmitted from missiles during their flight testing. They provide information about missile performance and important details about what the missile is carrying, such as how many reentry vehicles are being carried. These reentry vehicles bring nuclear warheads back through the atmosphere to their targets, so they are a measure of how many warheads are on a missile.

During the years of the START Treaty, a regular exchange of telemetry data took place to confirm the maximum number of reentry vehicles with which a given type of missile had been tested. This information, as already described, defined the counting rule for each missile: if a missile had released a maximum of ten reentry vehicles in flight tests, it was considered to carry ten warheads.

The new treaty was not going to depend on these counting rules, however, but on confirming the number of warheads directly through declarations and reentry vehicle on-site inspections. The U.S. military was firmly supporting this change because the U.S. Navy in particular wanted to solve the problem of overcounting of warheads on submarine-based missiles. Our job was to explain to the senators this complex issue, the upshot of which was that exchanges of telemetry data were not needed in the new treaty for the same purpose they had been needed in START.

The senators were also looking for assurance that the other streamlining we were looking at—in the inspection regime and the conversions and elimination regime—was not going to cost us confidence. Again, our job was to explain that we were looking at the changes to START not to suit the Russians but because our side had an interest in them too. We had heard loud and clear from our military services that they were concerned about the costs of elimination procedures and the operational interruptions that were happening because of inspections. We had to carefully explain these U.S. military interests to the senators.

We were not wholly successful. Both Senator Feinstein and Senator Kyl continued their grilling over several sessions in three days, and they were both tough questioners. The senior negotiating team did a good job answering, but part of the problem was that the procedures were just taking shape, therefore we were still a bit blind about what was going to end up in the treaty. From that perspective, the senators played a powerful role in steering our direction, especially on telemetry. Senator Feinstein was particularly determined that telemetry measures should be part of the new treaty because they had been such a central player in the success of START, its predecessor.

Senator Kyl also telegraphed his strong concern about the budget for the modernization of the nuclear triad and fissile nuclear material production. We in the delegation stayed on message about the value of a new treaty for U.S. national security, emphasizing the need for continued "eyes on" the Russian strategic nuclear forces through a new verification regime. It was clear, however, that Senator Kyl had some concerns that would have to be addressed before he would be willing to vote for the treaty.

Senator Kyl also reiterated concern for an issue that was already in play —missile defense. Separate discussions were going on with the Russians to try to develop an agenda for cooperation on missile defense, and a number of senators wanted to make sure that those talks were not going to turn into a new negotiation to constrain U.S. missile defense technologies and that the START follow-on treaty would not incorporate limits on missile defenses. The presidential statement from July had raised some eyebrows because it recognized that there is a relationship between missile offense and defense. It seemed I was wrong that a simple statement of fact on that matter would be noncontroversial. That issue followed us through the negotiations and straight into the ratification fight.

The lunch with the Russians was strange and interesting. Anatoly Antonov had organized a private dining room at a restaurant looking out over Lake Geneva, but it was clear once again that the senators were not there for a convivial chat but to ask tough questions. Perhaps not used to tough questioning from their own legislators, the Russian military men in particular bristled and, before long, we were into a big debate. The undercurrent was that the Russian Federation gained more advantage from arms control measures than did the United States.

There was not much I could do to steer the discussion, but I thought it was a good thing that the frank views of several Russian generals were clearly on display. They did not embrace the idea that the Russian Federation had an advantage, and they complained loud and clear about what they saw as U.S. attempts to gain military superiority, especially in using missile defense. At least nobody stormed out; at the end of the lunch, there were handshakes all around. Antonov reminded me that his own parliamentary delegation would be arriving in a few days.

Good to his word, Senator Kyl declined opportunities to socialize with us, but Senator Feinstein and her husband kindly organized a dinner for the delegation leadership on the night before they left. They reserved a table at Perle du Lac, a lovely restaurant right on the promenade overlooking Lake Geneva. Despite her unrelenting questioning of the previous two days, Senator Feinstein was a relaxed host; she and her husband wanted to know everything about everybody—families, dogs, where we grew up, you name it. I remember it being an evening when everyone, including the Senate staffers who are usually not prone to it, relaxed. Several bottles of local wine helped.

WARNING SHOTS ON RATIFICATION

When we got feedback from Washington regarding the senators' stay in Geneva, it was clear that the visit had been valuable in showing that we were ready to consult in good faith with the National Security Working Group and anybody else on Capitol Hill who wanted to know about the START follow-on negotiations. It was also clear what issues were going to be front and center, however, and telemetry was prominent. Senator Feinstein conveyed her concerns to Ellen Tauscher, and we got the word in Geneva that we would have to ensure that telemetry was included in the final document. Even if it were not needed to verify the treaty, it would be essential to gain Senate support for its ratification.

The visit of the National Security Working Group was an important watershed for the delegation. We went from being concerned only about dealing with the Russians and getting what we needed into the treaty to focusing on what would be needed for the ratification debate. It was also a wake-up call for the White House and the rest of the interagency team in Washington because they began to see the issues that would shape the debate, especially Senator Kyl's demands for more resources for fissile material facilities and nuclear weapon systems. The president would be considering nuclear modernization in any event during his administration, but Senator Kyl accelerated that process.

I believe that this early warning was important in shaping preparations for our work on Capitol Hill, but it was vital, in the end, in shaping the final treaty. Thus, Senator Nunn's call in 1980 for a Senate that was better able to give advice on treaty matters definitely bore fruit in the New START Treaty. The visit of the National Security Working Group was only the first step, however. We would have much more work to do with individual senators once the treaty went up to Capitol Hill for the ratification process.

NOTES

1. Foreword, "Report of the Senate Arms Control Observer Group Delegation to the Opening of the Arms Control Negotiations with the Soviet Union in Geneva," Switzerland, March 9-12, (III) 1985. I am indebted to Nickolas Roth for a thorough history of the group. See his "The Evolution of the Senate Arms Control Observer Group," posted June 5, 2014, Federation of American Scientists, www.FAS.org.

CHAPTER 7

LOSING THE RACE TO DECEMBER

FIRST MULLEN-MAKAROV MEETING

With the senators' departure, we turned immediately to preparing for the high-profile meeting of the chairman of the Joint Chiefs of Staff, Admiral Michael Mullen, with General Nikolai Makarov, the chief of the Russian General Staff. It was already near the end of November, and several major breakthroughs—including agreeing on numerical limits, the centerpiece of any nuclear arms reduction treaty—had not happened. Keen to get the treaty finished by mid-December, Washington was amping up pressure. We on the delegation agreed with the White House that we needed some high-level intervention to break through resistance and accelerate negotiations.

Mike Elliott, the senior Joint Staff representative on the delegation, was instrumental in getting Michael Mullen to come to Geneva. Mike worked with Vice Admiral James A. "Sandy" Winnefeld, the U.S. Navy three-star in charge of Joint Staff strategy, plans, and policy, to encourage Mullen to invest his time and reputation in an uncertain high-level meeting in Geneva. While the Pentagon had been very responsive and creative in solving various negotiation issues, we all feared that the Russian military bureaucracy would move too slowly in Moscow, putting up resistance every step of the way. After weeks of working with the Russian general officers on the delegation, Mike concluded that it was vital to get the two top military leaders together because their ability to establish a task-focused professional bond could help overcome institutional resistance in the Russian military establishment.

On the Russian side, it turned out that Antonov had similar fears about the U.S. military bureaucracy, so we agreed pretty easily that it made sense to get the two men together. November 23 was scheduled. Then the question came, how to organize the day to make maximum progress?

My long-standing view is that people work better together when they have a chance to have a meal together too, so I scheduled a dinner for the delegations at my apartment overlooking Lake Geneva. The day itself would involve two plenaries, one at the U.S. Mission and one at the Russian Mission, and opportunities for smaller side meetings, particularly between the two principals. If they were going to be able to help us break through on issues, they needed to get to know each other better and develop some rapport.

To me, this kind of structure made sense in terms of both protocol and pragmatic progress. As a result, I was surprised when I got pushback from the White House: the view coming at me was that we had no time for diplomatic niceties; we should meet all day long and into the night as necessary to make the final breakthroughs on the treaty. Central limits, the issues surrounding the offense-defense relationship, telemetry measures, and verification details such as unique identifiers on missiles should all be agreed in the one encounter.

I was not convinced that the two men, who had met only a few times in person, would be able to accomplish all these breakthroughs in the time available. I saw their visit as a vital catalyst for both our own work in Geneva and in the capitals. They could not deliver on every issue, but they would make it possible for us to finish the treaty in the coming few weeks.

I broached the idea of a nonstop day-and-night negotiating session with Antonov, and he shared my skepticism. In particular, the idea of not having a meal together seemed very foreign to him: we had to eat, didn't we? And he too thought that it would be a good thing if the two men got to know each other better, not only for negotiation of the treaty but also for the wider military relationship.

In the end, we came back to the idea of an intense day of plenary and smaller meetings, followed by a dinner in the evening. A large delegation arrived from Washington, DC, which included Michael McFaul and Gary Samore, the influential White House team who were our link to the president; James Miller, the principal deputy undersecretary of defense for policy; and Sandy Winnefeld, to provide senior support to Admiral Mullen.

In what turned out to be an important staff coordination pattern, Mike had been providing a constant stream of weekly updates to Winnefeld and Mullen over the months; he personally briefed Mullen on our progress each time he returned to DC. It was therefore not serendipity that both Winnefeld and Mullen were steeped in the negotiation issues that we were confronting; we had to move very quickly that day. Mullen's talking points for the first plenary meeting zeroed in on detailed questions such as the number of inspections that should be carried out—we were insisting on twenty whereas the Russians were insisting on sixteen, but they had already come a significant distance from their initial proposal of twelve inspections. We hoped that we could split the difference and come to agreement on eighteen. All the talking points were designed to make progress on the details.

Makarov had something else in mind, however. His talking points were expansive and returned again and again to big issues that would not be resolved in this treaty. The offense-defense relationship was an excellent example. He had a speech to make, and he was going to make it. He did not seem to have making detailed progress in mind.

The unflappable Michael Mullen was disposed to be patient and listen, but not so the others who had joined the U.S. delegation. Michael McFaul asked for the floor and clearly stated President Obama's goal of completing the treaty in short order, urging an immediate return to pragmatic issues that needed to be addressed. This sharply delivered message clearly did not go down well with Nikolai Makarov, so the first morning plenary meeting ended on a decidedly cool note.

When we returned to the SCIF, it was Sandy Winnefeld, now more familiar with the give-and-take of the negotiations, who quickly took the reins to develop a new script to get the most out of the afternoon meeting. Having worked with Mullen for some time, Winnefeld reduced the complex points to their essence and made them easy to get across—never forgetting that they would have to go through an interpreter, and so had to be as straightforward as possible. Mullen was resolved to make progress that afternoon so the trip would not be wasted.

I was very grateful to Sandy Winnefeld and to Mike Elliot who worked by Winnefeld's side answering immediate questions about substantive issues. I was afraid if we did not make progress, then the chairman might wash his hands of the negotiations, which would make it difficult, if not impossible, to finish the treaty and get it through the ratification process. It was quite a sight, a three-star admiral sitting at a classified terminal banging out talking points—but Sandy Winnefeld knew what needed to be said on the substance and knew how to get it across in Michael Mullen's voice.

Mullen decided to cut down the participation in the afternoon session, and so we asked the Russian delegation for a smaller meeting before a second plenary session—just the principals plus three others. That cut out some of the members of the U.S. delegation, and there was a fair amount of angst over it, but I think in the end it was the right decision. Mullen was able to connect with Makarov and get his points across, and I think that Makarov finally understood that he would have to take some responsibility for making progress in the negotiations.

The difficulty was that Makarov, unlike Mullen, was not yet immersed in the issues, and so he was not ready to make specific trades. Thus, although Mullen pressed him on the substance, in the end we did not get the catalytic effect for which we had hoped.

After some serious stocktaking in the delegation late in the afternoon, Mullen offered to give me a ride to my apartment for the dinner. I was glad to have the chance to talk with him quietly, and he took advantage of the opportunity to ask me some questions about how I saw the next few weeks unfolding. Once we got to the apartment building, however, he was not ready to take the rickety 1920s-era lift, so he headed up the stairs on his long legs. I tried to keep up as best I could, but I was not in the same shape as the chairman of the Joint Chiefs of Staff. Panting, I made it to the seventh floor some minutes behind him.

The dinner was not as comfortable as I had hoped: it took up every inch of space in my apartment, and there was not much room to stand and circulate among the tables. A small number of formal toasts passed between the delegations but did not deteriorate into the steady exchange of toasts that can so often occur with the Russians—I think they find it safer to express themselves in toasts than in private conversation. Toasts can be useful signals, but they are not a good way to get to know someone. Mullen and Makarov were hitting it off in conversation, I was glad to see, despite having to talk through an interpreter.

The best sign was that Makarov and Mullen agreed to meet again—in the morning, before departing—and whenever necessary to bring the negotiations to a successful conclusion. I breathed a sigh of relief. Not only would the chairman of the Joint Chiefs of Staff remain engaged, but his counterpart had pledged to do so as well.

This readiness was confirmed the next day, when the two senior military leaders summarized the discussions and laid out the agenda of issues that still needed to be worked. It was the exact list we had started with: the central limits of the treaty, the offense-defense relationship, telemetry measures, verification details such as unique identifying numbers for missiles, and numbers of inspections. We had not solved any issues, but we had agreed on what were the main ones and their priority. To me, this was an important accomplishment: it gave the Russian delegation's military members a high-level boost within the Ministry of Defense for working the issues, for they had clearly encountered resistance on some topics such as telemetry. Now, the chief of the General Staff was paying attention and had embraced these as his issues.

Mullen again invited me to ride with him, this time to the airport, and we had a serious discussion about how we were going to get the treaty done in the few weeks remaining before START went out of force. I broached with him for the first time the idea of doing a short, relatively simple treaty with the central limits and other main points agreed, but with the details of the verification regime left for later negotiation. It was an approach that had been used in the past, in fact in the negotiation of the INF Treaty, and I thought it would be a good way to complete a document for the presidents to sign before START went out of force on December 5. Given our experience with Makarov the preceding day, I was rapidly coming to the conclusion that it would not be possible to complete all the verification regime details by that time.

Mullen was properly noncommittal—it was my first time trying out the idea, and it had not been discussed in Washington. At the same time, he was supportive of the delegation and all the work that we were doing in Geneva, and he offered to help in any way he could, whether with his Russian counterpart, or with his senior American counterparts. I was glad to have the chance to thank him in person for sending to the delegation a top-notch team—from his senior representative, Mike Elliott, down to the most junior military member, the Joint Staff group was superb and effective.

THANKSGIVING

Then Thanksgiving was upon us, and I had a lot of homesick people on my hands. Many wanted to go home, but with the pace of the talks, we just could not take a break—and Washington wouldn't hear of it. Some of the defense experts invited their wives to come over, but everyone else was marooned without family. Before everybody descended into a funk, we decided that we'd better have a proper Thanksgiving, all together.

I had the biggest apartment around, and we had just proved with the Mullen-Makarov dinner that we could cram a big crowd into it. This crowd would be even bigger, however, so I was going to have to figure out some complex geometry, find more tables and chairs, and pray that the neighbors downstairs did not call the police. This was no joke. The Genevois are famously touchy about noise in their apartment buildings, so touchy that there is a city ordinance against flushing the toilet after 11:00 p.m. Luckily, just downstairs from me was Marcie Ries, the senior State Department representative, so I was sure she would join the celebration and wouldn't complain. I could also raid her apartment for tables and chairs.

Next, I approached Antonov. We had promised each other that we would pick up the pace, and indeed the working groups were meeting every day and sometimes twice a day, and he and I were meeting regularly in our particular format. I hated to be the one to say we needed a break, since it had taken the Russians time to come up to speed. Nevertheless, when I told him that we would like to take Thanksgiving Day off, he said "*nyet voporosa*" (no question that we should do it). I did not tell the White House, figuring everybody would be off for the federal holiday. That was a mistake.

When November 26 arrived, I had help from some of the men on the delegation to move furniture around: couches, chairs, end tables, and lamps all got stacked in the bedrooms. Tables and chairs came upstairs from Marcie's apartment, and we figured out how to fit everybody into the space. In the end, I had gotten permission to use the small efficiency apartment across the corridor from mine, which the State Department also owned and was being used for storage. We opened wide the doors of both apartments and set up tables in the little apartment as well as in the corridor. We managed to put in place enough seats for everybody.

The other problem was the oven in my swank European kitchen: very high-tech, but no way big enough to fit a Butterball turkey. U.S. missions abroad always order a big supply of frozen birds for their diplomats during the holidays. Marcie again came to the rescue: she had a normal American stove downstairs in her apartment, so I stuffed the bird and trudged downstairs to get it into her oven. We did a turkey breast in my oven, and somebody else had an oven big enough for another Butterball.

My first arrival in mid-afternoon was William Hopkins, one of our master interpreters, who had offered to do a centerpiece. I thought he'd put in place a modest creation with some flowers and berries, but Hopkins brought the makings of a giant cornucopia: fruits, vegetables, leaves, flowers, and the basket for them to spill from. It was gorgeous.

By late afternoon, everyone was arriving, and everybody brought something to eat that reminded them of home, or something to drink —the champagne flowed freely. We set up the buffet around the long kitchen counter and were in business. It being a diplomatic household, I had extra plates and silver, and some came upstairs with Ries—no paper or plastic for this celebration. There were two dishwashers upstairs and one downstairs to cope with it all.

I don't remember eating anything, but I am sure I did. Midway through I stood up to make a toast. I hadn't written anything down, but I just told everyone how grateful I was that we could all be together and how much I understood the sacrifice they were making by not being with their families on this most American of holidays. I thanked them for all the hard work they were doing and expressed my confidence that we would finish the treaty and get it to the president for his signature. I told them the president surely appreciated what they were doing.

While we were beginning to wash dishes—I have never had more willing helpers in the kitchen—my phone rang. It was the White House. Michael McFaul wanted to talk to me about how we were going to cope if START went out of force but the new treaty wasn't ready yet. It was obvious that he was working even if neither I nor my delegation was— the din in the background made that clear. I said I'd finish the cleanup and call him back shortly.

When I called him back, both he and Gary Samore were on the line, grilling me about how I was going to get the treaty done. It was obvious their subtext was, "Why aren't you in the office today? We are." I figured with the time difference they might have been in the office for a few hours but were likely going home to Thanksgiving dinner by 4:00 p.m. I didn't say anything, though. Their line of questioning was hostile, and I would have made them madder.

I was upset. Whatever residual glow there was from the dinner had disappeared. By this time, it was 10:00 p.m. in Geneva, and I called my husband in Virginia. It was 4:00 p.m. there, and the family was just starting to arrive for our usual gargantuan feast, this time without me. Ray is a natural host and doesn't get stressed when two dozen people are arriving and he has to take a crisis call from his wife. I paced up and down the kitchen and told him what was happening. He calmed me down and told me he would call back the next day while I was in the office, so we could talk longer.

Ray was a lifeline on this occasion, but as the situation got stickier, I didn't like calling him on either my mobile or my office phone. Both were open lines that I was sure the Russians were listening to. They knew that there were spats between Geneva and Washington—they had their own tough customers to deal with back in Moscow—but I did not want to let them know that I had critics in high places. The Russians could take advantage of such vulnerability, so I couldn't afford to let them see any.

For that reason, I asked Ray if he could find a secure phone in the State Department office where he worked. Unlike my arms control policy bureau, secure phones were scarce in his bureau, which handles the oceans, environment, and science. He had to use the single one available, which sat in his boss's outer office. I would agree on a time to call, and he would let the secretary know that he'd be stopping by to use the phone. She must have thought it strange that he was talking with his wife on a secure line, but we were not discussing the grocery list. We were discussing heavy weather in Geneva.

Ray has always been there to talk me through the tough times. An experienced negotiator and longtime Washington hand, he always comes up with some common-sense idea that I had not thought of. Oddly, I needed his advice to deal more with the Americans than the Russians. As for the Russians, I had their number. Ray had no need to know the substance of the negotiations; what I needed were his people skills: I couldn't always grasp the dynamics of what I was dealing with among my own colleagues.

December Tantrums

One of the major developments after that first Mullen-Makarov meeting in Geneva was that the White House decided the president should become more directly involved in the negotiations. Obama had already met with Medvedev in Singapore on November 15 during an Asia-Pacific Economic Forum (APEC) meeting, and the two men had pledged to stay engaged in order to keep up the pace of the negotiations and make rapid progress. Such high-level engagement is always welcome news for negotiators. It means that the talks cannot get stalled in bureaucratic morass in either capital. We could count on getting the instructions that we needed when we needed them.

Within days of the Mullen-Makarov meeting, President Obama was on the phone with President Medvedev to discuss one of the thorniest treaty issues: how to handle telemetry. Senators Feinstein and Kyl had both made their concerns known on this matter when they got back from

Geneva, and the president dove into the arcane issue with a lawyer's eye for detail. President Medvedev is also a lawyer; he too did not shy away from working the issue.

Twice in early December, the two presidents wrestled with the issue, trying to find a way through the conundrum that telemetry was not needed in the new treaty in the same way it had been needed, to confirm the counting rule, in START. At first very resistant, the Russians came to realize that an exchange of telemetry data would serve a useful transparency role, and had a political benefit for the United States: it would ensure a smoother ratification process in the Senate.

I was regularly hearing in Geneva that if we needed a political fix to smooth ratification, the Russian side would need one too. Now President Obama started hearing the same from President Medvedev, who wanted to put more on missile defense into the treaty text. We had continued to beat back that issue in Geneva and had succeeded to a significant degree. Antonov had early on declared that until we defined the relationship between offense and defense, we would not be able to reach an agreement. He and his delegation also tried to insert multiple references to missile defense into the treaty draft text.

We were able to beat back each of the issues at the negotiating table, but that did not mean the Russians stopped trying. They took the issue to the highest level and linked it to telemetry. In that way, President Obama also began to know more than he probably wanted to about the missile defense issue.

By early December, it was clear that we were not going to complete the treaty by the time that START went out of force on December 5. For this reason I had written to Washington, proposing that the presidents sign the treaty and perhaps its protocol but leave the detailed verification procedures for annexes that the presidents would then task their delegations to complete. Achieving this goal would be difficult because we still had not agreed on the central limits of the treaty and other top-line details. The protocol was also not finished, and I knew my delegation was nervous about getting it finished within a few days. However, remembering the history, I felt the option was feasible if both presidents decided that they wanted to go that way. Antonov and I had discussed it too, recollecting the INF precedent.

I was surprised, however, when President Medvedev proposed the idea to President Obama in one of their early December calls. I am not sure if President Obama had heard about my idea, but his instinct was to say no: the treaty, its protocol, and all the annexes had to be finished as a package so that they could be sent together to Capitol Hill for the ratification process. We needed to keep driving the pace to get the whole thing over the finish line.

Antonov was clearly angry with me afterwards. He said he had gotten Medvedev to raise it, why had I not delivered Obama? I reminded him that we had discussed it as an idea that would take some work in both capitals before the presidents could agree to it. I expressed my own surprise that he had taken the idea forward to his president's desk when it was still not ripe.

At that point, I decided that we would not finish in December. There was too much detail work on procedures still to be done, and my president clearly wanted that work to be completed before he would agree to sign the treaty. My efforts to communicate this fact to Washington, however, precipitated an explosion and crisis in Geneva.

After that presidential phone call, I wrote a note back to Washington proposing that we would keep driving forward in December but should also be ready to return to Geneva to complete the verification regime and other technical issues in January. Antonov had already conveyed to me that the Russian delegation would have to return to Moscow in late December to consult with the Ministry of Defense about what would be acceptable in the inspection regime, what they would propose for conversion or elimination procedures, and what they would be willing to accept in the telemetry realm.

I duly shared this information with Washington and, before I knew it, I was summoned to a secure videoconference with Deputy National Security Advisor Thomas Donilon. He was angry and wanted to know who had given me permission to break off the negotiations. I told him that I saw it as a natural step, after pressing so hard for the past several negotiating rounds, that the two sides would have to return to capitals. Both delegations needed to work through with their interagencies the details of ideas that had been developed in Geneva, and we needed technical information from the Department of Defense to back them up. Besides, I said, the holidays were coming up at the end of December for us, early January for the Russians, and people naturally wanted to be home with their families.

Donilon reacted furiously, demanding that the U.S. delegation stay in Geneva and continue working, holidays or not. Shocked, I said as gently as I could that the Russians would be leaving in any event, and I could not hold them at the table. Donilon replied that in that case, the U.S. delegation must stay at the table, work through Christmas, and make it clear that we were not the ones delaying the completion of the treaty. Furthermore, he said, from now on, my team and I would take a videoconference call twice a day from Gary Samore, the White House coordinator for arms control, to report on what we had accomplished in the morning and afternoon sessions of negotiation.

My senior negotiating team and I were reeling after that conversation, not sure exactly what to make of it. One thing was clear: the reality of the negotiations that we were experiencing in Geneva was not understood in Washington. I wanted to return to Washington, DC, with the team to work on how to fashion some compromises to break through the final issues. We could see what needed to be done to get to an agreement, but we could not convince the U.S. interagency at a distance. The Russians were in the same situation.

There followed about a week of twice-a-day "stand-and-deliver" video-conference calls, when each of my senior negotiators had to account for what he or she was doing. They were asked repeatedly what they were trading for specific items, which seemed to me a serious misperception of how negotiations work. Trades are not made on a piecemeal basis, but rather they take shape as part of package deals, some of which take days or weeks to develop. It was painful and extremely time-consuming to prepare for the calls, ironically taking away from the time we needed to prepare for the negotiating table.

I considered in that week tendering my resignation, but I knew that the goal of getting the treaty done quickly would be lost: bringing in a new chief negotiator and getting that person up to speed and into the action would take considerable time, a month or maybe more. The senior team also backed me up strongly: they did not want to see me thrown under the bus, they told me. We agreed among ourselves that we would stay through the Christmas holidays, but we told everyone else that they could go home to take a break with their families. If we had to sit it out in Geneva, we would not make everyone else do so.

Ellen Tauscher came to the rescue. She went to Secretary Clinton and conferred with her about how to remedy the situation. Secretary Clinton then went to the White House and talked President Obama through what was happening in the negotiations, where things stood, and what we could accomplish with a resumption in January: President Obama would get the completion of all the treaty documents, including the protocol and implementing annexes, as he wished. But the delegation needed to come home in order to prepare for a productive new round.

President Obama evidently agreed, because I received a phone call from Tauscher shortly after, telling me that there would be no more twice-a-day videoconference calls; the delegation should prepare to end the session later in December and to return to Washington, DC. In the meantime, she stressed, we needed to drive as hard and fast as we could to make as much progress as possible. I was extremely grateful to Secretary Clinton and to Ellen Tauscher. All the members of my delegation breathed a sigh of relief; we would be home for Christmas.

Putin Docks In

Ironically, the Russians were at last coming forward with important compromises, which I attribute to Makarov's new eyes on the negotiations. In the second week of December, they made a significant proposal on the verification regime, agreeing at last on eighteen inspections (up from the twelve they had initially proposed), the right to reinspect at bases that had already been visited in a given year, and not to insist on inspection of missile defense interceptors. One might ask why we would not want to encourage them to inspect missile defense interceptors—they would use up their precious inspections without getting to see our submarine, bomber, or ICBM bases. The answer, of course, is that we wanted no principle established or precedent set that we were limiting missile defenses.

The Russians also heard out our proposal for a non-deployed limit on missile launchers, which they had originally proposed. We took a long time to understand the idea, and in frustration, I think, the Russians took it off the table again. We eventually proposed a twist, however, which was to make two total limits, one on deployed delivery vehicles and the other on deployed and non-deployed launchers, to give them—and us—some flexibility to move launch systems in and out of deployment status. We would not have to count the launchers as deployed, for example, when they were going through maintenance. The U.S. Navy was especially enthusiastic because Trident submarine long-term maintenance can be difficult to forecast.

The main point, however, was to ensure that the Russians did not have extra mobile missiles stashed in garages that they could deploy quickly in a treaty-breakout scenario. If they were limited in the number of non-deployed launch systems they could hold, this problem would go away. In essence, we were limiting the breakout potential of the Russian mobile missile force.

It was clear in this productive period, a few days in the first half of December, that the Russians were prepared to speed up the resolution of issues. Antonov indicated to me that he had some flexibility, and the Russian delegation put forward a number of proposals on knotty problems, including telemetry. This to me was a good sign because they had mightily resisted doing anything on telemetry; they had waited on our proposals and never offered any ideas of their own. This too seemed to be changing. Indeed, the pace was so quick that I thought it possible to finish the major issues by the time we broke in late December and then plan to sign the treaty in early 2010.

That was until the Russian National Security Council meeting in Moscow in mid-December. I understood that Antonov expected to get the final go-ahead on a number of solutions to the difficult problems with which we had been wrestling. He promised to be in touch after he got the results—it was a weekend, but we intended to meet and prepare for a busy week, where we expected to get a lot of work finished.

Instead, on Saturday we got word that the Russians wanted a special plenary session at the Russian Mission in Geneva. During that session, Antonov read talking points that not only negated recent progress—for example, the eighteen inspections—but also took back some items that had long been agreed. We sat in stunned silence for a moment, and then I lost my temper. These are major steps backwards, I said, and are not at all in tune with our presidents' agreement to move forward steadily and in good faith to get the treaty done. As always, Antonov gave as good as he got. It was daring of me to question his president's good faith, he shot back.

After a few more sharp exchanges, we broke off the session and returned to the U.S. Mission. We immediately convened in our secure conference room to take stock. Negotiations are often one step forward and two steps back, but this had been ten steps back and no steps forward. We thought through what progress we could salvage and prepared ourselves for a tough week ahead. I thought for the first time that maybe it made sense to get the two presidents together again, to try to break through some of what to me was stubborn institutional resistance in Moscow.

I never knew what exactly happened, but in the end came to believe that it was not institutional resistance so much as the beginning of a power struggle over the treaty between President Medvedev and his prime minister, Vladimir Putin. Putin had not up to that point appeared to be interested in the negotiations, but later I heard rumors that he had suddenly come into that December Russian National Security Council meeting and simply crossed through all of the compromise proposals. Whatever the reason, we no longer had a fast track to resolving the major issues before the end of the year.

The START Bridge

At the same time all that was going on, we were looking for ways of addressing the demise of START. As early as November, the White House had formulated the idea of a "bridging agreement," a short politically binding agreement under which the two sides would pledge not to begin a buildup beyond the central limits of START and to continue some of the verification provisions of START. We wanted to ensure that the mutual transparency that we had become used to would continue while we finished the new treaty.

From the outset, however, the Russians were not keen on the idea. Moscow evidently saw it as a way for the United States to continue garnering the benefits of START without having to work hard to get the new treaty done. According to Antonov, Moscow foresaw nothing but delay from the United States if they allowed some temporary agreement to be put in place.

The Russians also raised doubts about the legal status of such an agreement. According to them, they needed a full, legally binding treaty, duly approved by their State Duma and Federation Council, in order to override their domestic law and permit foreign inspectors. According to the Russian state security law, no foreigners are allowed in sensitive nuclear facilities. A treaty can override that domestic law.

The same critique applied to other ideas that Washington tried. Senator Lugar, for example, in alliance with a number of senators on Capitol Hill, proposed putting in place new legislation to continue elements of the START Treaty on the basis of U.S. domestic law. The Russians were not willing to undertake their own new legislation in this vein, again arguing that it would be an excuse for the United States to delay completion of the new treaty.

In the end, we negotiated a short political statement, very simple, conveying the message that the United States and Russia would continue to abide by the spirit of the START Treaty while the negotiations for a follow-on treaty were continuing. It did not contain any notion that we would continue the verification regime, although we continued to press for exchanging at least some notifications as a goodwill gesture. The Russians remained staunch in insisting that verification measures could only be conducted pursuant to a legally binding treaty.

We issued the statement on December 4, 2009, the day before START went out of force, accompanied by some confident statements to the press that the negotiations for a follow-on treaty were continuing apace. They were indeed, and I was confident that we would get there, but not without some painful episodes.

In looking back on that difficult period, I think that I was helped by knowing the history of nuclear arms control treaty negotiations since their beginnings in the early 1970s. I knew that on one occasion, the president and chairman of the Politburo had signed a blank sheet for the television cameras, because there had not been time to finish printing out the treaty for the signing ceremony. The treaty itself was signed quietly not too long after. I knew that treaties had been signed without all of their implementing documents finished. In the end, the work had been finished, the treaties ratified, entered into force, and implemented.

Moreover, I knew that high-level individuals often took ownership of phases of negotiation, including presidents themselves. That is a good thing because it precipitates the final breakthroughs. I came to understand, however, that when high-level individuals decide to get involved, they do not always understand how best to achieve their objectives. Fair enough: when a president is breathing down your neck, the stakes are high, and you do not suffer gladly the people who have been struggling with the issues at the negotiating table.

Looking back, I also understand that I could have communicated better with Washington. I sent back my "negotiator's notes" almost daily, but often I did not get any feedback. I am not sure they were going beyond a narrow audience at the top of the State Department. Our routine reporting had fallen behind due to the press of work, so normal technical cables were not getting out as quickly as they should. Our "special cable channel" had been set up only at the beginning of November, and I am not sure everyone who should have had access had been given it, especially in the White House and Department of Defense. So, in many ways, I understood the genesis of the difficult episode, but that did not make it easy for me or my senior negotiating team.

As it turned out, both Antonov and I were suffering. He confided to me on returning to Geneva in February, after the December trip to Moscow, that for the first time in his life, his blood pressure had gone sky-high. He had been put on medication and almost had not been cleared to return to the negotiations. I appreciated his candor, but I did not tell him that while I had been home in Washington, DC, I too had been diagnosed for the first time with high blood pressure and put on medication. I too had had some work to do to get my medical clearance to come back to Geneva. So the talks were taking a toll on both the chief negotiators.

CHAPTER 8

COPENHAGEN—
THE PRESIDENTS MEET

STRANGE ENCOUNTER IN A DRESS SHOP

No doubt the greatest asset to the New START negotiations for us and the Russians was the willingness of both presidents to engage. In December, Obama and Medvedev had already had multiple phone calls; they were both extremely knowledgeable about the treaty issues. They even got to joking to each other about telemetry. After the debacle of the Saturday plenary session, I thought immediately about the global summit on climate change in Copenhagen, coming up within a few days. The presidents were supposed to meet there, but on the wider agenda of the "reset" of our relations. I asked Washington if we might also use the occasion to try to recover ground after the setback.

President Obama, of course, had to be willing: he was focused on success in the climate negotiations as part of his larger agenda. We could not expect him to focus on the treaty all the time. In this case, however, he was willing, and the White House players—General James Jones, Gary

Samore, Michael McFaul—were also very supportive. They asked me to make plans to come to Copenhagen to be there for the meeting.

Antonov had the same instructions, so we both went to work to make arrangements—no mean feat since Copenhagen was bursting at the seams with the climate delegations, flights were scarce, and he needed a visa to travel inside Europe. Somehow, our executive secretariats made it all happen; it was not the last time I had cause to be grateful to the executive secretaries, Karen Kirchgasser and Sergei Rudenko.

The Copenhagen climate conference of 2009 is famous as a difficult meeting. The Danes had just built a new conference center, and it was not yet through its shakedown cruise. It was surrounded by a sea of mud because the landscaping had not yet been finished. Most important for us, meeting rooms for heads of state and government were scarce, and the U.S. Embassy in Copenhagen had to work hard to scrounge up a space for the presidents' meetings.

The result was the strangest space that I have ever seen for a high-level meeting. When I saw it, I burst out laughing. It was a clothing shop in the basement of the convention center. All the clothes had been shoved along racks and were hidden behind curtains, along with twenty stark-naked mannequins. I have to give the embassy and the organizers credit for creativity because the actual meeting space was dignified: two rows of couches facing each other, two armchairs for the principals at the front, chairs for the interpreters, and the usual flags and flowers.

I arrived first with my embassy escort and sat quietly waiting. Soon the White House team arrived, but I was not expecting to see the president immediately: I thought he would wait in a holding room somewhere until the meeting began. But the president did arrive, and Michael McFaul took me over to introduce me. I have to say I wrung President Obama's hand with probably too much enthusiasm—I was thrilled to meet him. We took our seats to wait for the Russians while I chatted with General Jones and Gary Samore about some of the technical details that were before us. I noticed that the president was quietly watching me, appraising me. Little wonder since he had been hearing complaints about me in the past couple of weeks.

I was glad that Secretary Clinton was there with President Obama; we spent some waiting time talking about the status of the negotiations and what my expectations were for finishing them up. She asked me what she could do to help, and I told her how grateful I was that she had helped us work through the difficult period with the White House. She was keen to know how she could help us to drive forward faster, and I was glad that she was ready to be involved with Russian Foreign Minister Sergei Lavrov, always a rough customer, to keep the pressure on.

When the Russian delegation arrived, it included Sergei Prikhodko, Russian Assistant to the President, as well as a team from the Ministry of Foreign Affairs, and, of course, Anatoly Antonov. The presidents immediately got into discussion and were able to agree with relative ease to the central limits of the treaty that we had been struggling over for months: 1,550 deployed warheads and 700 delivery vehicles. We had some discussion of the separate limit on deployed and non-deployed launchers, but since the Russians had temporarily taken it off the table, we did not spend much time on it. We would resume that battle later on.

We quickly bogged down, however, on the long-standing tough issues: unique identifiers for missiles and bombers, telemetry, and how Russian concerns over missile defense would be handled in the treaty. Medvedev was also not ready to return to the compromise over the number of inspections that the Russians had given and then taken away.

I loved watching the two men negotiate. They obviously had a good rapport. Both of them are lawyers, and they easily grasped the issues and need for balance but also precision. President Obama was obviously frustrated that he could not break through on more issues, but I think that President Medvedev was stepping cautiously as he tried to balance the need to get the treaty done with his prime minister's sudden interest and delay tactics.

After about an hour, the presidents were scheduled to go on to other meetings but Jones and Prikhodko stayed behind to continue the discussions. The two men had met a number of times, including in Moscow in July, and had a good working relationship although they were from very different backgrounds—Jones from the military, and Prikhodko from the diplomatic service and the Kremlin. They did not make much progress on substance, but they agreed that we needed to keep driving the pace quickly and broached the subject of another meeting between Admiral Mullen and General Makarov early in the new year.

When those meetings were over, my presence in Copenhagen was no longer needed. President Obama and Secretary Clinton went on to a dramatic climate fight that lasted until the early hours of the morning, but I went back to my hotel room, wrote up notes, and fell asleep exhausted. The next morning, I flew back to Geneva. Antonov was on the same flight.

The very next day, December 19, was a Saturday, and we had our wrap-up plenary meeting at the U.S. Mission before breaking off the round to return to our capitals. I had decided to keep it short and simple because we both knew where things stood after the difficult week just passed. Antonov, however, could not resist a lengthy exposé of the current status of the negotiations, which mostly accorded with my own and so did not require too much comment. He obviously needed to fill the airtime, I suppose for recordkeeping with Moscow, but the rest of us were fairly numb by the time it was over. The main importance of that plenary session, in my view, is that he and I agreed in the margins to sustain tight communications throughout the interregnum, to be ready to pick up the mobile phone whenever it rang. This proved to be important.

Most of my delegation headed home that day or Sunday, but a few of us stayed behind to make sure that all the reporting from the round was out the door. It also gave me some quiet time to think about next steps. One of them that I quickly woke up to was that it was almost Christmas and I had not given a single thought to the family or to gifts. Slightly panicked, because Geneva is not an easy shopping town unless you have a taste for high-end goods, I grabbed an hour to go to my local supermarket.

Luckily, Carrefour had a range of kitchen equipment, some socks and underwear, and plenty of chocolate and gourmet foods for sale. My husband and sons made do with Christmas gifts from the supermarket that year. I am glad to say that although the chocolate is long gone, the kitchen gear is still in use in the family households.

Putin Ups the Ante

Once all the cables were out the door, I finally got on a plane to fly back to the United States, only to encounter the first of two enormous snowfalls in Washington, DC, that winter. The runways were plowed at Dulles Airport, but the gate areas were not, so we waited for a couple of hours to disembark. By the time I finally arrived at home, I was glassy-eyed. It was December 22.

The holiday week passed quietly, but on December 29, before I went to bed, I checked with my research assistant about what the Russian press was looking like. Olga, a native Russian speaker, was a graduate student at Georgetown University, and she had been sending me a "press take" every day from the Russian-language media. This had been vital because it helped me keep up on the internal politics and interagency dynamics in Moscow.

On this occasion, she had alarming news. Prime Minister Putin had been out in the Russian Far East that day to open a pipeline and take part in some other events. In a tough speech before a youth group in Vladivostok, he had ripped into the START follow-on negotiations, claiming that the treaty being worked was weak and inadequate because it did not constrain U.S. missile defenses. TASS and InterFax, the Russian press agencies, reported the speech prominently on their news wires.

When I read the reports, I was jolted. That's the end of the negotiations, I said to myself, and asked Olga to do a compilation overnight of what I assumed would be a wave of negative stories out of Moscow the next day. Then I went straight to bed, overwhelmed by fatigue and disappointment.

The next morning, I was wide awake at 5:00 a.m. and opened up the message from Olga with dread, expecting the worst. To my surprise, she told me that there were no further stories about Putin's speech in Vladivostok. Quite the opposite, she said: when she checked the TASS and InterFax websites in the middle of the night Washington time, where the original reports had been, there was only the notation, "This story has been taken down."

I was amazed. Someone had decided to stand up to Prime Minister Putin and insist that he not blow up the negotiations. I can only assume that that person must have been then president of the Russian Federation, Dmitry Medvedev. I know that there is general skepticism that President Medvedev ever defied Prime Minister Putin during his time in the presidency. I am convinced, however, that he did so on this occasion.

Immediately I called and reached Antonov on his mobile in Moscow. He was properly circumspect on the phone, but he readily agreed with me that we had to move swiftly to nail down the schedule for the next Mullen-Makarov meeting, this time in Moscow. I suggested early January, but he said that the Russian delegation could not possibly be ready before the third week in January—this was understandable both because they had significant interagency work to do and because Moscow shuts down for two weeks for the New Year's break.

I told him I would have to check on the acceptability of the dates for the chairman and the rest of the senior team in Washington. He pledged to do the same, and we promised to be back in touch to confirm dates before New Year's, which is Russia's biggest family holiday. It was December 30.

That day I spoke to the senior people in the White House, to James Miller and Mike Elliott in the Pentagon, and to my own leadership in the State Department. Everybody agreed, with some reluctance, that the third week of January would work—definitely there was a strong preference to go earlier, but it was clear that our hosts would not be ready for us. Now we just needed Mullen to agree that he would be willing to go on those dates. His staff had already told me that his calendar could be cleared for the trip.

I asked Mike Elliott's advice on how best to broach it with the chairman, and he recommended calling Sandy Winnefeld for help. Winnefeld was on a ski trip with his family in Colorado—the one time in the year he took any time off—so with reluctance I undertook to call him. His communications team said they would relay my request and get back to me as soon as possible. We were getting ready for a New Year's party at home, so I went off to do the grocery shopping. I had not managed to do any up to that point, and I felt a little like the lawyer in the classic "Miracle on 34th Street," who has to race off to Christmas shop after failing to prosecute Santa Claus. The holidays were upon us, and there was nothing I could do to stop them.

And so it was that Sandy Winnefeld's communicators found me in my car in the parking lot of the Whole Foods Market in Falls Church, Virginia. Winnefeld was actually in a lift line on the ski slopes when my call came in, but he heard me out and agreed quickly that he would contact the chairman himself.

Within a few hours, we had an answer back: Admiral Mullen was willing to go to Moscow in the third week of January. I let the Washington team know that we had a date, then called Antonov back and confirmed that we would be in Moscow on January 23. We promised to stay in touch through the holidays concerning the agenda and arrangements; he promised not to put away his mobile phone. I breathed a sigh of relief and relaxed just a little for our New Year's party.

I recount this tale because it's an excellent illustration of how much priority this issue was commanding in the Pentagon and with the chairman himself. Sandy Winnefeld and James Miller were always ready to help, and they had a great team in Geneva, Mike Elliott, and Ted Warner, who kept them updated on all the details. This strong DOD support is one of the core factors, in my view, in the success of the New START Treaty negotiations.

The rest of that holiday season was a blur because we were planning for the meeting between Admiral Mullen and General Makarov, and we had quite a bit of coordination to do, up to and including with President Obama. The issues, especially telemetry, were ones with which he was familiar, but we also still needed to nail down one of the central limits of the treaty—on deployed and non-deployed launchers, the breakout barrier we were proposing. Thus far, in Copenhagen, we had only agreed on the deployed warhead limit (1,550) and the delivery vehicles limit (700). On the verification front, we knew that we wanted some extra inspection measures related to mobile ICBM bases, but we needed to be clear about what our proposal would be. And we still did not have agreement on the number of inspections or on the use of unique identifying marks on individual missiles.

Within a few days of New Year's, the deputies were meeting and then the principals—the cabinet secretaries under the chairmanship of National Security Advisor James Jones. One wrinkle developed when it became clear that Secretary of Defense Robert Gates did not want Admiral Mullen to go to Moscow without unequivocal top cover from the White House. It had to be clear that Mullen had the full support of President Obama. Thus, General Jones agreed to join the delegation in Moscow.

Throughout this period, I kept getting indications from Antonov in Moscow that missile defense would be a big topic of conversation on the Russian side. I warned him not to hang up the negotiations on the subject because we were prepared to make progress—and fast. We would not, however, be prepared to negotiate about missile defenses in this treaty. I did stress to him, however, that there would be people along on the delegation who would be ready to talk about missile defense. My boss the undersecretary, Ellen Tauscher, was leading on missile defense cooperation with Russia, and she was coming to Moscow with the team. She was ready to talk with her counterpart at any time—but separate from our negotiations.

Although never spoken about, I kept getting indications that Prime Minister Putin's blast in late December against the negotiations was continuing to reverberate. One was Antonov's constant reminders that missile defense had to be part of the negotiations: this seemed to be Prime Minister Putin's central issue. Another was a Russian reluctance to come back to Geneva: although we pressed them hard at every level, they did not want to return to the negotiating table until February 1. They clearly had a lot of stresses and strains to deal with in Moscow.

As for the U.S. side, we were prepared to make progress when we arrived at Andrews Air Force Base on January 22, 2010, to take military air flights to Moscow. I traveled on the plane with General Jones, Ellen Tauscher, and the White House team, Gary Samore and Michael McFaul. Admiral Mullen had his own plane, and the Pentagon people traveled with him. Sandy Winnefeld and Mike Elliott were there from the Joint Staff, and James Miller and Ted Warner from the Office of the Secretary of Defense. Other team members had to travel commercial, but all the agencies were represented at a senior level, and all my Geneva members, including Marcie Ries, Dick Trout, and Kurt Siemon, were there. It was a big delegation, a lot of firepower, and we were determined to get as much agreed in a day of negotiations as we possibly could—even though we were stopping for a banquet at midday.

Figure 1. Megan Gottemoeller standing with son Dan (7), holding son Paul (3).

Source: Arnaudo family album.
Note: My nieces Megan and Hillary Gottemoeller joined me in Geneva in summer 1990 to watch Dan and Paul while I worked on the START delegation. Here they are on an excursion, Paul flagging, Dan still raring to go.

Figure 2. Ambassador Anatoly Antonov, a worthy opponent.

Source: Courtesy of the United States Mission Geneva.
Note: Anatoly Antonov and I spent many hours wrangling over the treaty text and solving problems between our delegations. He was a skilled diplomat and worthy opponent.

Figure 3. First press conference with Antonov in Rome, April 2009.

Source: Photo from the Associated Press (AP Photo 090424010818; Alessandra Tarantino).

Note: Ambassador Anatoly Antonov and I held our first meeting at the U.S. Embassy in Rome on April 24, 2009. Afterwards, we held a brief press conference to announce the start of the talks.

Figure 4. The two delegations gathered in front of the Russian Federation Mission Geneva.

Source: Courtesy of the United States Mission Geneva.
Note: The two delegations are mixed up together in a group shot in front of the Russian Mission in Geneva.

Figure 5. The "hear no evil, speak no evil, see no evil" shot presented to President Obama on the day the treaty was signed in Prague, April 2010.

Source: Courtesy of the United States Mission Geneva.
Note: My favorite photo of the delegation—we were all relieved and happy that the talks were coming to a successful close.

Figure 6. The official delegation photo presented to President Obama in Prague, April 2010.

Source: Courtesy of the United States Mission Geneva.
Note: The formal portrait of the delegation, still smiling but not so exuberant. I would be happy to be in a foxhole with any of these people.

Figure 7. The six senior delegation members with President Obama at Prague Castle, April 2009.

Source: Courtesy of the Barack Obama Presidential Library.
Note: The delegation has a moment with President Obama before the signing ceremony at Prague Castle on April 8, 2009. From left to right: Richard Trout, Michael Elliott, Ted Warner, President Obama, myself, Marcie Ries, and Kurt Siemon.

Figure 8. Presidents Obama and Medvedev shake hands after signing New START.

Source: Photo from the Associated Press (AP Photo 10040818738; Petr David Josek).
Note: Official photo at signing ceremony.

Figure 9. With Vice President Joe Biden, Secretary Hillary Clinton and Senate Foreign Relations Chairman John Kerry.

Source: Courtesy of the U.S. Senate Photographic Studio.
Note: I convince Vice President Biden, Secretary Clinton and Senate Foreign Relations Chairman Kerry on a final point in the Resolution of Ratification for the New START Treaty. This was one of the worst moments of my professional life.

Figure 10. Family photo following the Senate vote on the New START Treaty, December 22, 2010.

Source: Courtesy of Cecile St. Julien.
Note: A happy moment for my family; I was glad that we could all be together. From left to right: Ray Arnaudo, Paul Arnaudo, me, Dan Arnaudo.

CHAPTER 9

JANUARY REGROUP IN MOSCOW

MULLEN AND MAKAROV MEET AGAIN

One of the great prides—or perhaps vanities—of American diplomacy is that U.S. negotiators are able to get off the airplane after a night flying across the ocean and go straight to work in a different time zone. There have been some exceptions. Henry Kissinger insisted when he was negotiating with the Israelis and Arabs that the talks would have to take place on his time, even if it was in the middle of the night in the Middle East. But then, he was Henry Kissinger.

For the rest of us, the myth is that you will get some sleep on the plane, but that is impossible. For one thing, you are too keyed up. For another, your colleagues and bosses want to keep talking about tactics and substance. For a third, if you're on a certain older type of military air flight, the plane must stop for refueling in Newfoundland, Iceland, or Ireland. In that case, of course, you have to deplane lest it blow up while refueling is going on. I learned long ago not to succumb to the

Irish coffee at Shannon Airport. It had the effect of further keying me up and giving me a terrific headache at the same time.

We arrived in Moscow on January 23, ready for action. It was bitterly cold in Moscow and snow was on the ground, but we spent much of the next twenty-four hours inside the Ministry of Defense. I was impressed that we were ushered upstairs to the main meeting halls of the ministry itself, rather than to the separate protocol building reserved for foreigners. The Ministry of Defense is impressive in its late Soviet style—a lot of gilt, mirrors, large frescos, and heavy drapes. Where furniture is concerned, however, the ministry has a taste for something lighter: delicate chairs in Louis XV style.

Our first meeting was with the Chief of the General Staff, General Nikolai Makarov, in his office—also a significant signal that our negotiations were important enough that we weren't being treated as "normal foreigners." It was good to see that the working relationship that had developed between General Makarov and Admiral Mullen in Geneva was paying off: they greeted each other heartily and agreed to get right down to work.

The setting was not ideal. We started out in an enormous plenary session with about twenty people on each side of a massive table—our large delegation and their equally large one. It was good to see that the Russian interagency was well-represented—Antonov waved at me across the expanse of polished wood separating us—and the rest of the Russian delegation was either at the table or on the back benches. Such formal settings and large groups are usually not a recipe for progress. Nevertheless, it was a way to get started.

Mullen and Makarov both read their opening statements, and I breathed a sigh of relief because it was clear the Russians had done a lot of work since we parted in December. The eighteen inspections that they had given us in November and then taken away were again in play. They seemed ready to talk about all other topics that we wanted to talk about—unique identifiers on hardware, the limit on deployed and non-deployed launchers, telemetry. I listened attentively in both Russian and English to hear what they would have to say about missile defense, but surprisingly there was not one word.

The Russians were keen to hear what we had to say about verification measures regarding mobile missiles, based on their insistence that mobile missiles should not be treated any differently than other mobile launch platforms—submarines and bombers. Here we did not have much to say because we were still working out the issue in Washington. We were, however, ready to talk about the bomber-counting rule. Would they be ready to move beyond the START rule, which counted one warhead for each bomber? That would require some on-site inspection at their warhead storage facilities on their bomber bases—something they had always resisted in the past.

Within two hours, the two military leaders agreed that we should break into smaller groups to try to work some of the difficult issues. I asked my senior negotiators to take the lead on the issues for which they were responsible—Mike Elliott on the bomber-counting rule and unique identifiers, Ted Warner and Dick Trout on elimination and inspection procedures, and Kurt Siemon on telemetry. Again I was questioned by the White House—why wasn't I circling among each of the working groups?

I explained that the reason was straightforward—the senior leads knew the technical details and I did not. They could make faster progress than I could—and certainly they would make faster progress without me interrupting them. Antonov and I were there to help them if needed, but our main responsibility in the negotiations was the treaty text, which was not in play that day. These more technical details would go into the protocol or the annexes, and we would then clean up the treaty text to match them.

At lunchtime, we broke for a banquet in an elaborate dining hall. I ended up surrounded by Russian generals—two of them, Generals Orlov and Poznihir, I knew, but not most of them. We had some very entertaining conversations about nuclear policy and force structure. I think that they were quizzing me to see if I really did understand the issues. Mostly, though, I think they were just bemused that a lady could talk their language.

The banquet was hurried, with a minimum number of toasts—only Admiral Mullen and General Makarov got up to speak. The generals surrounding me were not drinking, although per the Russian style there were two different wine glasses, a champagne glass, a shot glass for vodka, and a cordial glass at each place. Each glass could have been filled if we had asked, but luckily no one did. To me, this was an added sign that the Russians meant business. Instead of forcing a lot of drinks on the jet-lagged Americans, they were ready to get back to the negotiating table as quickly as possible.

And so we did. We spent a considerable amount of time in the afternoon plenary session on the notion of a third central limit in the treaty, on deployed and non-deployed launchers. We wanted to set it at 800, just one hundred launchers more than the delivery vehicle limit of 700 that had been agreed by the presidents in Copenhagen. In that way, we would be able to ensure that the Russians could not build and store an unlimited number of mobile missile launchers—any that they did build would have to be counted as part of the "non-deployed" limit. Such a limit would also give us flexibility: bombers being converted to conventional roles would not have to be counted as deployed, nor would submarines that were in overhaul.

As I described earlier, the idea had been hatched by the Russians—we had seen it first in their early draft of the treaty tabled in September. However, we were not crazy about the rest of the draft, which featured a loose approach on verification. Honestly, we didn't really understand the importance of the non-deployed launcher limit until later study. The Russians had therefore taken both the draft and the launcher limit off the table. At the plenary meeting table that January, they teased us a bit about it, wanting to hear why we thought it was so important. In the end, Makarov accepted the 800 limit with a flourish and a smile. He enjoyed hearing us ask devoutly for something that they had offered and then withdrawn. To me, it was the biggest breakthrough of the meeting.

The second big breakthrough that afternoon came on unique identifiers, which the Russians had resisted as imposing extra burdens on them. Who was going to take responsibility for painting new numbers on the missiles and keeping track of them? This time, however, we brought an entirely sensible proposal: we each had already assigned serial numbers to our missiles and bombers, for our own tracking and maintenance purposes. We proposed that we simply make use of those existing national numbers, which are unique to each piece of hardware. The Russians, after some discussion among themselves, agreed.

These unique identifiers have proven to be a major innovation in the success of the New START verification regime. When inspectors arrive at a base, they receive an update on all systems that are located at that inspection location. The systems are identified by their unique numbers, which appear in the big database to show where every missile, bomber, and launcher is located at the time the complete data set is exchanged on a six-month basis. These unique identifiers also appear in every notification of missile, bomber, or launcher movements, and the other side must be notified of every movement.

This allows us to track the Russian strategic nuclear forces on a 24/7 basis. The Russians, in the same way, can track the movements of our strategic nuclear forces. We both know what missiles are being refurbished, which ones are returning from maintenance, and which ones are being moved to new bases. This day-in, day-out snapshot of the status of each other's nuclear weapon systems is a real breakthrough for predictability and mutual stability—an innovation in the New START Treaty.

When we wrapped up the negotiations in the evening, we had a real feeling of accomplishment. We had come a significant distance on a couple of key issues, and we were also congratulating ourselves that missile defense had not dominated the conversation. In fact, it had not even come up. I concluded that Antonov had some high-level political players breathing down his neck, but for whatever reason, the Ministry of Defense was not so concerned about the missile defense issue. I was looking forward to the opportunity to rag him about it.

At the same time, there was some bad news for the traveling party: Admiral Mullen and General Jones planned to leave that very evening, taking most of the senior delegation members with them. However, General Jones' plane broke down at the airport, and it would be some time, perhaps a day or two, before spare parts could be brought in to fix it. The national security advisor could not afford that kind of delay, and so Admiral Mullen asked him to travel on his plane. That meant a volunteer had to remain overnight and travel by commercial air the next day: Sandy Winnefeld agreed to do so.

And so Winnefeld ended up with a little time to explore Moscow, where he had never visited. He and Mike Elliott went to take a walk around Red Square, accompanied by Lani Kass, senior advisor to Admiral Mullen and a Russian speaker. It was a bitterly cold night, and Winnefeld had not come prepared with an overcoat since he had been planning to go straight back to the airport after the day's talks. Navy guys are tough, however. As they were strolling Red Square, a little old lady, the inimitable Russian babushka, came up to Winnefeld and started laying into him for not being properly dressed. Kass translated; "You'll catch your death," was apparently the least of what she had to say. I would have been glad to be there: a four-foot-high grandmother berating a six-foot-five Navy admiral. Winnefeld did survive unscathed, both the babushka and the cold.

BREAKTHROUGHS? NOT SO FAST

The next morning, the rest of the delegation went off to the airport to fly back to Washington, DC, but I stayed behind because I wanted to make sure that we both had the same understanding of what had been agreed. We had not taken the time to write everything down and get both sides to agree to it, and that always made me nervous where the Russians are concerned.

Before their departure, I had worked with my senior team to write a short description of the agreements that had been reached—unique identifiers, the number of inspections, the central limit of 800 on deployed and non-deployed launchers. We also described some progress on telemetry that Kurt Siemon had been able to accomplish working with General Poznihir and his missile experts, and some discussion of the bomber-counting rule that Mike Elliott had led. I did not mention missile defense in the paper because it had not come up at any time during the day.

While the delegation headed off to the airport, I proceeded to the Ministry of Foreign Affairs for a meeting with Antonov in his office high above Moscow. When I walked through the door with my embassy notetaker, the first thing out of Antonov's mouth was, "Don't think that because missile defense wasn't raised yesterday, it is not important." I smiled and replied that I was indeed surprised given how he had been so insistent that it would be a central theme of the discussions. He then stated that indeed it had been raised in a private exchange between General Makarov and Admiral Mullen. I again expressed surprise because the two military leaders had not had a lot of one-on-one time—perhaps a brief conversation might have been possible, but not a major intervention. Before turning to focus on what had been accomplished the previous day, I commented that I would check on the issue with Mullen's staff when I returned to Washington, DC.

I handed Antonov my short summary, which is something we call a "non-paper" in diplomatic parlance—a document for discussion, but not an official proposal. I started to go over it, and that is where the trouble began. Almost nothing that we had written down on the U.S. side as "agreed" had been so remembered by the Russians. Antonov again tried to insert missile defense, but I underscored that it had not in fact figured in the talks, so it could not be a part of the meeting outcome. The meeting broke up in short order, and I went back to the U.S. Embassy, puzzled and worried.

I wrote a report back to Washington and waited, for the delegation was still in the air. I knew once they landed and digested my report they would not be happy, because we all believed that we had made significant progress and created some real momentum to finish the negotiations quickly. The senior White House people, Gary Samore and Michael McFaul in particular, were beginning to sense a victory for President Obama's arms control policy, and they were pleased by what we had managed to accomplish.

Indeed, the reaction to my report was swift and negative. It was one of several occasions when, as the messenger, I felt full of bullet holes. Reflecting on the incident, I think that Antonov was trying to serve two masters—his president and his prime minister. Prime Minister Putin had already been making it publicly clear for a number of years that he worried about U.S. missile defenses and the effect they might have in undermining Russian strategic nuclear forces. Would the United States, with a perfect missile defense system, finally be able to engineer a perfect first strike against Russia? President Medvedev, for whatever reason, was not so worried, and he certainly had not become publicly invested in the issue the way Prime Minister Putin had. Most interesting to me was the fact that the uniformed military did not seem particularly concerned about it—perhaps because they understood the full capacity of the Russian ICBM force to avoid or undermine an attempted U.S. first strike.

Luckily, the main breakthroughs that we agreed during the second Mullen-Makarov meeting in Moscow were reconfirmed when the two delegations reconvened in Geneva in February. Several stiff exchanges between the two capitals were required to set things straight, but the Russians confirmed that they were ready to accept a launcher limit of 800, and they confirmed that they were ready to use preexisting numerical designators as unique identifiers on the delivery systems. The number of inspections stuck at eighteen. The bomber-counting rule was agreed soon after. Telemetry, however, took a good deal more work and became an important endgame issue for the negotiations.

The other endgame issue that took shape after Moscow was the treatment of mobile missiles in the verification regime. The Russians were insisting that the special mobile missile measures were unique to them and therefore represented a bigger burden for Russia in the verification regime—going against the basic rule that all measures should be reciprocal in nature. They also insisted that mobile missiles represented no greater a verification problem than other mobile launch systems, such as submarines and bombers.

For our part, we needed to fix several problems that had emerged in START. The Russians had taken to flushing mobile missiles out of their deployment bases once they had received word that the inspectors were headed to a certain base. The START Treaty allowed them to do so. Thus, we needed to tighten the time between when our inspectors arrived at the point of entry (POE)—Moscow or Ulan-Ude—and announced which base they would be inspecting and when they got to the inspection site. We also needed to directly limit the potential for Russian mobile launchers to leave the inspectable area once the inspection had been called. These proved to be difficult endgame issues too.

And we could not escape missile defense, which Antonov kept insisting had to be a greater part of the treaty than we could agree. To me, it became increasingly clear that there was a political imperative driving this issue, rather than military necessity. Nevertheless, it proved extraordinarily complex to resolve, and not without a few additional bullets coming at me from Washington.

CHAPTER 10

THE LONG WINTER SLOG

LA BISE AND "SNOWMAGEDDON"

My reentry into Geneva did not bode well after a tense six weeks in Washington, DC, and the trip to Moscow with Admiral Mullen. I tripped over the entryway in my apartment and fell flat on my face, much to the consternation of my colleagues who had picked me up at the airport. Luckily, aside from my pride, nothing was damaged, so I dusted myself off and got ready for the new round to start. It had to be our last: February had already arrived and President Obama had made it clear he wanted to sign the treaty as soon as possible, and certainly no later than a nuclear security summit that he was hosting in April.

My instructions were clear: get it done. Actually, when we resumed work that round, most of the major issues had been resolved. We knew what the treaty's central limits, including the new limit on deployed and non-deployed launchers, would be. We had agreed to a new method to count warheads and were working out the details of how we would verify it. We had agreed to a new concept of verification and the unique identifiers for missiles that would make it possible. We had agreed on the number of inspections and on how to exchange data.

But still open were several core issues: how telemetry and missile defense would be represented in the treaty, which the Russians had linked, how to conduct the conversion or elimination of certain weapon systems, and how to verify mobile missiles. We needed to ensure that we fixed several problems, especially the predilection of the Russians to flush mobile missiles from their bases once an inspection was called, taking them out of the area available for inspection. So it was going to be a difficult round, but I had every expectation that we would be able to get the treaty done.

The Russians too appeared to be in a better battle rhythm after their six weeks at home, and especially after the meeting between Mullen and Makarov. They returned to Geneva with good energy and, it seemed, a clear slate of instructions. In particular, they did not try to reopen issues that had been settled in the Mullen-Makarov meeting, which was good news for us: the stiff phone calls between Washington and Moscow had evidently paid off. Antonov did warn me that unspecified "political forces" were continuing to keep an eye on him and his delegation.

Mike Elliott was in charge of the conversion or elimination issue; he was very attentive to what we needed to get done, but he also had a lot of fun with it. In the START Treaty, there had been a number of detailed procedures for "C or E," as conversion or elimination was referred to. Once again, they had proven expensive to implement, and the Department of Defense wanted to simplify them. Bomber and submarine tube conversions had been especially difficult and had led to long, drawn-out discussions in the START implementation commission as to whether bombers or submarine tubes could be removed from accountability under the treaty.

This was the genesis of the so-called "phantom warhead" issue: although some of the older bombers had been taken completely out of service and scrapped, the Russians insisted that they could be resuscitated if the United States really needed them. Likewise, some of the submarine tubes had been filled with ballast and were no longer capable of carrying or launching missiles—but the Russians could not be convinced. They refused to take those bombers and missiles out of treaty accountability—the warheads still had to be counted, but from the U.S. perspective, they did not exist: they were phantom warheads.

For our part, we needed to ensure that the Russians were truly eliminating silos and the equipment associated with them, in addition to missiles. We agreed that we did not necessarily have to confirm every single elimination event with an on-site presence, but we also wanted to ensure that the systems that had been destroyed were displayed in such a way that our own national satellite systems could see them and thereby confirm the elimination.

Mike Elliott had the most fun with the constant Russian desire to hang onto equipment, putatively to convert it to other uses. The Russians, for example, proclaimed that they wanted to hold onto the "transporter-erector-launchers" (TELs) that were used to move mobile missiles around and raise them to an upright launch position. They said that they wanted to convert them into construction cranes.

Mike pointed out regularly that this converted crane would be no substitute for a purpose-built construction crane; no construction boss in his right mind would want to use one of them. He teased them when they insisted that they couldn't possibly leave the covers off of silos for sixty days so that our satellites would see the process of eliminating them. They complained that cows might fall into them. In that case, Mike said, you could use your converted cranes to haul the cows out of the silos. Eventually, the Russians fell off both issues.

The most detailed discussion was over the amount of space and time that could be allocated to display eliminated missiles and other treaty-accountable items so that our satellites could check the elimination. The Russians couldn't just strew eliminated equipment across a large base and tell us to go hunt for it with our satellites, then give us two days to find everything. Mike engaged in exacting discussions about how large the *ploschadka* or display area could be, and how many days items would have to be displayed. In the end, we agreed not only to the size of the area but also to how the eliminated items should be laid out within it and to a reasonable display time—60 days from the time that the display was announced. Both sides could also request an inspection to confirm the elimination within 30 days of the notification. All measures, of course, were reciprocal.

We fought long and hard over the conversion of bombers and submarine tubes, eventually agreeing to measures that confirmed the conversion of all the B-1 bombers to conventional-only platforms. The conversion of submarine tubes and the total elimination of the B-52 bombers proved to be more difficult, however. Eventually, Mike gained agreement on both issues, but some on-site inspection procedures were not fully worked out during the negotiations. They continued to dog us during the treaty-implementation process.

The C or E issues moved forward on a pretty steady track, but other issues did not. Ted Warner and his team were struggling with the issue of mobile missile verification because the Russians were adamantly trying to throw out everything that had been done in the past. We got their message loud and clear that they wanted a different approach, one that was not unique to mobile ICBMs, but we still needed to be able to monitor these systems that were forming more and more of the backbone of the Russian ICBM force. A lot of back and forth was going on between Washington and Ted's team as well as between Moscow and the Russian team, which was led by Colonel Il'in. It was an intense discussion, which was not making progress.

Likewise, Kurt Siemon was driving the telemetry issue with a lot of experience and a significant memory bank from the START negotiations. He understood what had been needed in START and why an exchange of telemetry was not needed in New START. At the same time, he was perfectly aware that telemetry had become a high-level political issue, which President Obama and President Medvedev discussed every chance they got. Kurt brought a highly knowledgeable technical team from

Washington, and they were instrumental in finding solutions. He did not have an easy partner in General Poznihir, who had his own great expertise on the issue and really did not think much of including telemetry in New START at all.

As for me, Antonov and I were struggling over the missile defense issue. With the political forces at his back, he was determined to get something on missile defense into New START beyond the language that we had agreed in the preamble. I was pushing back nonstop, but he was not budging.

We resumed the practice that we had begun in November of a regular heads-of-delegation ("HODs") meeting with the two of us and two notetakers, one Russian and one American, both bilingual in Russian and English. In this way, we could speak quickly and easily in both languages and cover a lot of ground in our discussions. We went over the main treaty text almost daily, to focus on areas where additional work needed to be done and to ensure both delegations were on the same page with regard to priorities. We also used the meetings for problem solving in the working groups; if our team leaders came to a halt in making progress, they would bring the issues to us to try to resolve.

It was in the HODs meetings where I learned that Antonov had an unexpected problem-solving side. He was well-known in Washington as a tough negotiator and wasn't much liked, because he could be nasty. He also, as I've recounted, loved to play games and from time to time did his best to make me look foolish. Nevertheless, we had developed a decent working relationship in the fall and that paid dividends now, especially given the strict marching orders in hand from our presidents to finish the treaty quickly. Antonov's most common expression in this period when we were trying to break working-group logjams was *"spravimsya,"* or "we'll work it out." He usually went back to his delegation and did work it out. I hope he can say the same about me.

About this time, *La Bise* roared in from the Alps and put Geneva into a deep freeze. The "bees," as we called it in English, is a violent wind that comes down Lake Geneva and can sometimes blow for days on end, summer and winter. It's one of those winds that is said to bring ill fortune or drive people mad. Although I can't say we had either of those problems, at least on the U.S. delegation, the cold and ice it brought on were remarkable. All the trees along the lake were iced up from the waves splashing and freezing. One unlucky Volkswagen parked near the quay was completely encased. For its owner's sake, I hope once defrosted it started up as quickly as did the 200-year-old Volkswagen in Woody Allen's 1973 film, *Sleeper.*

La Bise ushered in a period of colds and flu for both Americans and Russians, and delays started to build up in some of the work strands. There was nothing that could be done about it. The senior delegation leads carried a tremendous amount of knowledge in their heads and followed the progress—or lack thereof—from day to day in their working groups. They had also established their authority and working relationships with their counterparts, and no one else could step in. I have to say that on both sides, the leads got up out of bed as soon as they could. I never suspected that the Russians who were absent were slow-rolling us. They were ill.

Hard on the heels of *La Bise* came Snowmageddon, three feet of snow in two days. This was the second large snow event of the season in Washington, DC—the first had hit just before Christmas and delayed many of us on the delegation from getting home. Snowmageddon closed the U.S. government for a week. For us, Washington went dark just at a critical juncture in the negotiations: we were not getting any instructions, and we couldn't even talk to people on the phone. In those days, most government officials did not have secure telephones at home, as strange as that may seem in our current era of ubiquitous communications.

For me, this led to another big dustup with the White House. Antonov and I continued to talk about missile defense, and I continued to tell him that we could not add additional language, never mind limits on missile defenses, into the treaty. He continued to argue back that they too needed something for their political process in Moscow, just as in Washington we needed something on telemetry.

After a while, and with radio silence from Washington, I began to think about some of the joint statements that had been issued historically along with the signing of arms control treaties. Some have had important treaty functions, such as clarifying a procedure, but sometimes they had truly been declarations adopted to satisfy a political concern on one side or the other but with no treaty effect. I knew that many precedents exist in nuclear treaties—indeed, START had a significant share of them.

So Antonov and I started discussing the notion of a joint statement about missile defense that would accompany the treaty. I thought it was a good idea. If I could get the Russians to drop their demands for additional missile defense language in the treaty, which would be legally binding, and move their language to a joint statement, which would not be legally binding but would have political effect, it might solve everybody's problem.

Antonov and I tried out some ideas and hit on the model of a joint statement from the Adapted Conventional Forces in Europe Treaty (A-CFE). It conveyed that the signatories did not intend to build up conventional forces in Europe, but it also did not impose additional obligations on them. I sent the idea back to Washington as an example, for what I thought would be a discussion of the pros and cons of the approach. Somehow it landed on the desk of President Obama himself and made him extremely angry, because he evidently believed that I was freelancing unhelpfully. I heard about it before too long via another blistering phone call from Thomas Donilon. I thought I was truly done for as the chief negotiator.

Luckily, I had good support from the State Department. Secretary Clinton again stepped forward in my defense, as did the undersecretary for political affairs, William Burns, and my own boss, Ellen Tauscher, the undersecretary for arms control and international security. In Tauscher's office resided the secret weapon of U.S. arms control policymaking—the legendary James Timbie, a senior advisor to the undersecretary who for decades came up with clever ways to move forward in negotiations. I had first met him when he worked for Undersecretary of State for Arms Control and International Security Affairs Reginald Bartholomew in 1990. Twenty years later, he was still at it.

Timbie helped to calm everybody down, reminding whomever needed it about the role of side declarations or statements in arms control treaties. He also came up with a better idea than mine: instead of a joint statement, why shouldn't we think about two parallel statements? The United States would convey that its missile defenses were not designed to undermine Russian strategic offensive forces, and the Russians would make some statement acknowledging the U.S. declaration. It was classic Arms Control 101, and I was relieved that the White House quickly bought into the idea. The two statements were not easy to negotiate—it was one of the significant endgame issues—but the process succeeded in taking the steam out of the argument. We were on our way to a resolution, and both the White House and the Russians seemed happy.

Antonov and I turned our attention to cleaning up loose ends, and we spent days talking over the notion of new types and new kinds. "New types" was not so difficult, for precedents had been well set before in preceding treaties, including START. When a country is deploying a certain type of a missile, it can develop a next generation of that same missile and bring it under the treaty as a new type of an existing missile. Once the missile is ready to leave prototype status, the country offers to exhibit it to the other treaty party and declares it subject to the treaty limits. In this way, both we and the Russians were able to modernize our existing nuclear forces while keeping the new weapons within treaty bounds.

"New kinds," by contrast, are completely new weapon systems that have no predecessors in the treaty limits. They may be weapons based on new technologies, or they may be weapons based on old technologies but never before constrained in a treaty. For example, the Russians have been developing a new nuclear-propelled cruise missile, the engine technology of which has never been deployed before. For treaty purposes, it would be a new kind of weapon. Likewise, the United States has always taken a strict line about not bringing nuclear armed sea-launched cruise missiles (SLCMs) within treaty limits. For treaty purposes, if the United States were to build a new nuclear-armed SLCM, it would be a new kind, even though the technology is quite old.

Because Antonov had never had to deal with these issues before, we spent a long time just establishing the concepts. In Russian, the words were "*typ*" (type) versus "*vid*" (kind), and he could not seem to grasp the difference between them. Eventually, we sorted out that the handling of "new types" had been well-established in previous treaties and that we should just go with those precedents and procedures. He had no problem with that solution.

But we kept wrestling with what to do about "new kinds." I insisted that there needed to be a way to talk together about new nuclear weapon systems that might emerge during the life of the treaty, even if they would not be automatically subject to the limits of the treaty in the same way as new types. Antonov kept insisting it wasn't important, that he couldn't imagine it being a problem during the life of the treaty.

Eventually, we agreed that either of us—if we were concerned about a new kind of weapon system that was under development in the other country—could raise the matter and ask questions about it. Those conversations would take place in the Bilateral Consultative Commission (BCC), the implementation body of the treaty. However, for a new kind to be brought under the limits of New START, the country developing it would have to be willing to make it subject to the treaty.

In fact, the Russian Federation has developed a number of new systems during the life of New START—the hypersonic glide system Avangard; the heavy missile Sarmat; the air-launched ballistic missile Kinzhal; the previously mentioned nuclear-propelled cruise missile, Burevestnik; and the anti-ship missile Tsirkon, which has long-range, land-attack potential.

Knowing what I now know about these systems, I might have considered Antonov's long puzzlement to be a negotiating ploy, an attempt to throw dust into the works. However, the fact that Russia is ready to treat several of them as new types and bring them into New START belies that notion. President Putin and Foreign Minister Lavrov have officially said that Russia would be ready to do so with the Avangard and Sarmat,[1] and some Russians experts have said that Kinzhal also could come under the treaty if deployed in a certain way.[2] Only the Burevestnik and Tsirkon in this case would not be new types under the treaty, but they are not slated to be deployed until after New START goes out of force in 2026.

Noteworthy, too, is that the Department of Defense wanted to ensure that my negotiating position on new kinds remained constrained. The DOD was looking to protect the development of conventionally armed hypersonic glide vehicles (HGVs) and instructed me to inform the Russians that the United States would not bring its new conventional HGVs under the treaty. I dutifully delivered this message at a plenary session, thus making it a formal statement in diplomatic parlance. It's ironic that the Russians have since declared that they are ready to bring their Avangard HGV under the New START Treaty.

When I look back on the incidents that got me in the White House's crosshairs, I wonder if I acted too relaxed as a negotiator. As one of my Washington colleagues said to me, "We would see your smiling face on the videoconference screen and wonder if we were ever going to get the treaty done." In other words, I suppose that I was projecting good-natured calm but not a sense of urgency. Confidence in my ability to deliver, along with my delegation's, started draining away.

I certainly didn't feel relaxed—I was getting three hours of sleep a night and would spend the waking time staring at the ceiling thinking how to fix things in the treaty, or how to deal with colleagues on both sides of the table. From Geneva, I saw very few issues that needed to be resolved, but they did require some heavy lifting on the part of the backstopping team and the different departments in Washington. As a result, we weren't receiving instructions, and the forward motion in the negotiations stopped. I was getting frustrated, and so was my team.

A DEAL TAKES SHAPE

Now we were in a rush to get everything to come together. Antonov and I were both well aware of what movement was needed on each side, and to be honest, his side moved first. The Russians gave their final concessions quickly and waited for us to take our last steps to adjust our policy on mobile missile verification. It became clear to me, however, that we would not be able to work this issue through to conclusion in Geneva. Washington wanted to be involved.

This phenomenon is quite common in arms control talks. Indeed, during the endgame of the START negotiations, the senior U.S. and Soviet interagency teams, known as the "Un-Group," descended on Geneva and stayed there until the treaty was finished. I kept reminding my negotiating team of that fact, even as they felt stymied that they were not getting the instructions out of Washington that would allow them to make the treaty finally come together.

The Russians also were quite aware that this is how treaty endgames often work: the delegation is not able to take it over the finish line. Antonov was calm about it; if a negotiation is succeeding, he would say, the generals want to arrive and take credit—the foot soldiers get pushed aside. If the negotiation is failing, he would go on with a wry smile, then the foot soldiers are taken out and shot.

That is how Ellen Tauscher and James Timbie came to arrive in Geneva to make the final moves on the missile defense statements and finish up the mobile missile verification issue. Tauscher had a big personality and expansive manner, and I think she shocked the Russian delegation, particularly its military members, when in her first plenary meeting she went over to their side of the table and gave each of them a hug and a kiss. It was certainly a disarming move.

The main issue to be addressed—how to handle mobile missile verification—was front and center. The Russians wanted no special measures, but we were intent on ensuring that they could not flush the mobile missiles out of range of our inspectors once an inspection had been announced. This problem in START had led to many frustrated exchanges in the Joint Compliance and Inspection Commission, the implementation body of the treaty.

We knew that we needed to adjust procedures in order to shorten the time between our inspectors' arrival in Moscow or Ulan-Ude (the points of entry to Russia for the inspections) and their arrival at the base to start the inspection. That is because inspectors would announce to which base they were going when they arrived at the point of entry (POE). If the travel time from POE to base was long—and the distances in Russia are vast—then the Russians had plenty of time to move their mobile missiles.

We had actually been able to do a lot at the delegation level to shorten the time between arrival at the POE and arrival at the base. This work was facilitated by the considerable amount of discussion that had gone on earlier in the JCIC to try to fix the problem in START. When Tauscher and Timbie arrived, however, we had not been able to nail down specific restrictions on movement of the missiles, and we had been holding tight to the START procedures to use as leverage to get what we wanted.

The Russians were complaining loudly because they had given up their principal concessions earlier and their leverage was limited. However, they well understood the old negotiating adage that "nothing is agreed until everything is agreed." They began threatening that if we did not agree to measures that were acceptable to them, they would begin to unstitch other parts of the treaty and we would not be able to finish.

In addition to limiting mobile missile movements after the inspection had been called, we needed some way to determine the area where the missiles could be located and where they could not. Normally, they would be found close to their maintenance shops, refueling sites, and other support facilities. However, Antonov used to tease us regularly about hiding extra mobile missiles in the woods. Indeed, we wanted to stop them from doing just that.

It was delightful watching Tauscher browbeat the Russian military men, and they did not seem to know what to make of her. We tried a number of approaches, considering practicalities such as how to determine the roaming range of the missiles between refueling stops and how to structure site diagrams. As is often the case, in the end the fix was conceptually simple and straightforward: The missiles and their launchers, whether deployed or non-deployed, could only be located on their bases, except for limited transit periods. If mobile missiles were found anywhere else on Russian territory, they would be violating the terms of the treaty.

The final issue to be resolved in the negotiations was a small thing after so many months of blood and sweat. We on the U.S. side had to prepare a list of places where our bombers may be found out of area, that is, outside the continental United States without being permanently based there. That is because under the terms of the treaty, it is forbidden to base strategic offensive forces outside the territory of either treaty party. However, U.S. B-52 and B-2 bombers range widely and can be found in far-flung places such as Diego Garcia in the middle of the Indian Ocean. We needed to clarify for the Russians where the bombers might land for refueling or maintenance or mission activities without being permanently based there.

To her credit, Tauscher let me hand over this statement in our final negotiating session and then we all got up to congratulate one another. It was my birthday: March 24, 2010. As we shook hands, Antonov handed me a birthday gift from the Russian delegation: an enormous bouquet of roses. There was an odd number of them because gifting a dozen roses is bad luck in Russia. So even though I had begun the round with an unlucky fall across my threshold, I ended it in better grace with the gods of fortune. We would need it.

NOTES

1. Vladimir Putin, "Presentation of officers appointed to senior command posts," Moscow, November 6, 2019, http://kremlin.ru/events/president/news/61991; "Foreign Minister Sergey Lavrov's interview with Russian and foreign media on current international issues," Moscow, November 12, 2020, https://www.mid.ru/web/guest/foreign_policy/international_safety/conflicts/-/asset_publisher/xIEMTQ3OvzcA/content/id/4429844?p_p_id=101_INSTANCE_xIEMTQ3OvzcA&_101_INSTANCE_xIEMTQ3OvzcA_languageId=ru_RU.
2. See, for example, Alexei Arbatov interview, https://russiancouncil.ru/analytics-and-comments/interview/kontrol-nad-vooruzheniyami-nuzhno-vo-chto-by-to-ni-stalo-sokhranit-i-preumnozhit/.

CHAPTER 11

APRIL GLITTER IN PRAGUE CASTLE

GETTING IT RIGHT IN TWO LANGUAGES

Once negotiators agree on that final issue and shake hands across the table, then a treaty must be ready to sign—at least that's what the negotiators would love because by that time they are exhausted. But that is far from the reality. Every single change to the treaty text, including that final issue on the last day, cascades throughout the document and its protocol and annexes. Sometimes hundreds of small changes have to be made to ensure that the treaty and its whole package of subordinate documents are consistent. The same goes for the subordinate documents—if a change is made in a verification procedure in the protocol, then it cannot contradict or undermine the treaty. They must be consistent.

That is where conforming comes in. Conforming is the unglamorous but vital function of making sure that the treaty documents are consistent and that the English and Russian translations of the texts are identical in meaning. If differences in translation are missed, then they can lead to some uncomfortable surprises, such as when inspectors arrive at a base and find out the other side doesn't understand the procedure for inspection in the same way.

Conforming teams must be led by people who have an eagle eye for detail and are highly skilled diplomats. Often, they must push the other side hard to accept that the sentence in plain English can mean nothing else in plain Russian. Experienced Russian linguists are a critical part of the U.S. team, as are treaty lawyers. On the Russian side, they bring in their own treaty lawyers and experienced English linguists. At the end of the day, every member of the conforming teams must be able to confirm that the two texts are of equal meaning in English and Russian.

We were lucky to have one of our most experienced nuclear negotiators, Neil Couch, leading the U.S. conforming team. With him were our most experienced Russian translator, Victor Lychyk, and Marshall Brown, our most experienced treaty lawyer who also spoke Russian fluently. At Couch's advice, they started early, back in December when we thought that we might be signing the treaty and protocol at that time but leaving the implementing annexes until later. It was a good thing that they did because we had only three short weeks between finishing the negotiations and presenting the treaty to the presidents in Prague for an April 8 signing ceremony.

The Russians also had some internal procedures to go through, including getting relevant government ministries under then Prime Minister Putin to certify that the treaty was in the Russian national security interest. I know that Antonov was worried about getting all the required signatures in place before the Prague ceremony—even though President Medvedev was ready to sign it. At that time, it was unclear whether Putin would embrace the treaty as a good thing for Russia, although later he praised it as "the gold standard" of nuclear treaties.

Given the amount of attention to the treaty in Washington, I knew we had to come as close to a perfect, clean copy of the treaty as possible, even though that had not always been the case with the arms control treaties of the past. The START Treaty, once it was signed, had had more than

100 corrigenda, the legal term for corrections that needed to be made. Those were small edits, theoretically not substantive in nature, but they were necessary to ensure that all the parts of the over 600-page package —treaty, protocols, annexes—were consistent. After START was signed, a U.S. team had gone to Moscow and successfully worked through all the corrigenda, but I knew a process of that magnitude this time would not be smiled on by the Obama White House.

Gumbo and Easter

Easter holidays arrived and the rest of the U.S. Mission in Geneva took off, but we had to keep working—the signing ceremony in Prague was only a few days away. This was a problem because the cafeteria closed down and there were no food services within walking distance. How could I keep people at their desks without food? Everybody brought in snacks, of course, but luckily, I had a secret weapon in the delegation, and she had a big heart. Cecile St. Julien, or "Ceil" as everybody called her, was from Louisiana and an expert on cooking gumbo. Her Cajun relatives had sent out the right spices, so she volunteered to make gumbo for the entire delegation on Palm Sunday, a week before Easter.

I was amazed when the U.S. Mission chef stepped forward and said that he wanted to help—usually people in Switzerland value their holidays and don't give them up for anything. No, he explained, he had always wanted to make gumbo and here was a great opportunity to learn how. In addition, a couple of the Filipina ladies who were the usual servers in the cafeteria also volunteered. I don't know if they wanted to learn to make gumbo too, but they were willing to help.

And so, on Palm Sunday, we had a fantastic gumbo lunch, with the whole delegation taking it in turn as their working groups broke from meetings. I didn't make it downstairs until late in the afternoon, but there was still some left, and the gumbo team was basking in praise. I will never forget Ceil St. Julien's smile as she handed me a bowl. "We did it, Rose," she beamed. I didn't ask her if she was referring to the treaty, the gumbo, or both.

The good mood from the gumbo led everyone on the delegation to ask if we could have an Easter lunch together, just as we had celebrated Thanksgiving together in November. I was afraid we would need to work on Sunday, but I could see that we were close enough to having the treaty ready that we could take a break from meeting with the Russians. I talked to Antonov about it and to my surprise, he said that his delegation also wanted to celebrate Easter—the Roman and Orthodox calendars coincided that year—so yes, he would prefer not to have any joint meetings that day. He hastened to add that not everyone on his delegation would be observing Easter—but I was already thinking, "How un-Soviet."

Like at Thanksgiving, our Easter feast was potluck. Unlike Thanksgiving, though, we were able to use the big conference hall at the U.S. Mission, which was open to us anyway because everybody else was off for Easter. That made it easier, given how my apartment had been bursting at the seams at Thanksgiving and when Mullen and Makarov came to dinner. Some of the delegation offered to set up the tables and decorate, and everybody else brought their favorite spring dish, or wine and other beverages. The U.S. Mission chef, still willing to help us out, cooked chicken.

I don't remember what I brought that day, but I do remember it as the warmest, happiest time in our months together. The hard work of the negotiations was over, and we could see the treaty taking shape for the president's signature. Everyone, Christian or not, was feeling festive. We had a lot of fun with the toasts and jokes—we even had a "kids' table," where I sat. These kids were allowed to drink wine. The best thing, though, was the Easter prayer that Carolyn Pura, our experienced telemetry expert, wrote:

Easter Prayer

Father, we come before You today to celebrate a special week and a special place. We will look back on this coming week as the time when it all finally came together and the long-sought signature actually happened. We have worked hard together over the last six months, some longer, striving to do what we felt was right and have all realized at various times that we were participating in history being formed.

But today we also celebrate a heritage that transcends the historical moment in which we live. Our Jewish colleagues have celebrated Passover this week, a time when more than 3,000 years ago You delivered the Jews from slavery in Egypt by passing over their households, negating a death sentence in Egypt that would allow them to escape with freedom. And today as Christians, we celebrate the joy of Easter, with the death and resurrection of Christ freeing us from the slavery of the limitations of our own sinfulness. For our Catholic colleagues, we see the time of Lent come to a close today as they have experienced a time of sacrifice in honor and remembrance of the great sacrifice You paid. For our Protestant colleagues, we come together on Easter Sunday today in Geneva, the city where the roots of our understanding of God's grace toward us were developed by the likes of John Calvin and John Knox, as they sought to understand the extent of Your love. And this year the Russian Orthodox Church, a part of the tradition if not the practice of our Russian partners in this negotiation, is celebrating Easter today along with the Western Christian church.

As we enjoy this time together and the fabulous meal of which we are about to partake, we ask for Your blessing on the work we are finishing this week and ask that it may richly fill the purpose we have worked for.

The gumbo meal and Easter celebration showed me that the delegation had taken on the properties of a family—closely knit, shouting at each other some days, but sticking together no matter what. We had been through a lot, not only in the drama of dealing with Russians and

Washington but also in the day-to-day problems, sometimes crises, that we confronted. We'd had medical emergencies, big events back home —babies being born, kids getting into college, aged relatives to worry about—and we had held each other up through it all. I will be forever grateful that I had the chance to work with them, to be with them. They are all people whom I'd be glad to have beside me in a foxhole.

Prague Castle: The Presidents Sign the Treaty

Easter was on April 4 in 2010, and the signing ceremony was scheduled for April 8, four days later. On Monday, we sent off the advance party to Prague to begin producing the formal treaty document for the presidents' signatures. I was confident that Neil Couch and Marshall Brown would ensure that the right version of the treaty got from the electronic files to paper. This was no simple task: the treaty, its protocol, and the annexes had to be printed on formal U.S. treaty paper, which is a thick and beautiful bond that requires special printers to print. These printers and a supply of the treaty paper were arriving with a team supervised by Avril Haines, who went on to become Obama's deputy national security advisor, but on this occasion was the lead NSC lawyer who would ensure that the document was ready for the presidents to sign. The Russians had similar teams converging on Prague.

This final production might seem a bit much, but a treaty is among the highest legal documents of the land, and so it must be correct—or at least as correct as humans can make it at the moment of signing. Nobody likes corrigenda. As long as treaty paper abides by the standards of the nineteenth century, twenty-first century technology must adapt to it.

The printers were of twentieth-century technology especially designed to handle the thick paper, but they were clunky and inclined to break down, which is why several of them were brought to Prague. They needed their own software experts too because they had been invented in the era before Microsoft Word, when the State Department was still using Wang computers. I took regular phone reports from Neil Couch in Prague as to how everything was working, praying that the treaty would emerge from the printers unscathed and on time.

Another issue that emerged that week was whether anybody from the delegation would be allowed to attend the signing ceremony. Washington was not exactly ecstatic about our role, and I feared that we would be left to watch the ceremony on television in the U.S. Mission in Geneva. It was out of the question that the whole delegation could go, but I argued to the White House that at least the lead negotiators, representing each of the important agencies who had made the treaty happen, should be allowed to attend.

To his great credit, Michael McFaul stepped forward and made our case to President Obama, and by Tuesday we had gotten word from Washington: the lead team was invited to Prague. Marcie Ries, Ted Warner, Mike Elliott, Dick Trout, Kurt Siemon, and I all scrambled to get plane tickets. The embassy in Prague had booked the Marriott Hotel where the president would be staying and, luckily, there was room for us there.

A question then came to us from the rest of the delegation: could we take a gift to President Obama on their behalf, something to show our support for his work on nuclear arms control? We thought about it for a while and decided to present him with two photos: one, our official delegation shot taken at the end of the negotiations, and the other, decidedly unofficial. Before we settled in for the formal shot, the photographer caught us all talking, joking, pointing at each other—Karen Kirchgasser had her hands over her ears, Kurt Siemon had his hands over his mouth, and Ted Warner had his hands over his eyes. We called it the "hear no evil, speak no evil, see no evil" shot, and among all the photos taken of the delegation I like it the most: we're all laughing (see figures 5 and 6).

For a U.S. embassy anywhere in the world where the president is visiting, there are many headaches, but some are worse than others.

One is what to do with delegation members who only have to be in the president's "security bubble" for one or two events and then have no other duties. Such was the case with me and my pals from Geneva: we were in Prague for the ceremony but not for his other meetings. We did have to be available for a press briefing after the signing, however, so we couldn't just be shunted into Prague Castle and out again: we had to be moved to different places.

Late in the evening on April 7, I got the word from our embassy protocol officer: Be ready to go in our own van before the president started moving. If we didn't make the van, we would be locked down until after the president's motorcade left and we would miss the ceremony. So, early in the morning we got into the van and were off to Prague Castle. I'm not sure to this day why we needed to take the hairpin turns on the castle approach at such speed, but we raced into the courtyard with teeth rattling and were ushered upstairs.

Prague Castle inside is beautiful, glitter and crystal, paintings and glorious parquet. We were placed in a reception room and told to stay put: we were going to get an audience with the president. President Obama arrived a short while later and came in to see us. As in Copenhagen, I have to admit I probably gushed too much for the president's taste, but he listened kindly to my story about the two photographs, and I was able to stammer out how much the whole delegation supported his work. He took the time to speak with all six of us about our roles in the treaty. Then we posed for photos. I was glad that my senior team at last had a chance to meet the president, talk a bit about their work, and shake his hand. In the photos, we are all grinning (see figure 7).

Then it was time to move to the hall where the signing ceremony would take place. As I walked down the corridor, I bumped into Avril Haines, who had been in charge of producing the treaty for signature. Avril was carrying a large bundle of paper bound with ribbon between two leather covers. She asked me if I'd like to hold "my treaty" before the presidents signed it. I haven't been able to track down this photo, but that is how there came to be a funny picture of me standing in the hallway of Prague Castle, cradling the treaty as if it were my newborn.

The signing ceremony passed in a blur, but all went well. (See figure 8.) It's funny that my two sharpest memories revolve around the Russians. First, President Medvedev in his remarks said that the treaty was a "win-win" for both Russia and the United States. If you know the Russians, "win-win" is not part of their culture; they are a much more zero-sum kind of people: if you win, I lose, and vice versa. So for Medvedev to say the treaty was a win-win is a memory worth savoring.

The second incident involved Russia's treaty lawyer, also a woman, who stood behind President Medvedev. A senior lawyer always does this job, ensuring that the presidents sign in exactly the right spot, and for exactly the right number of times: in this case, once on the U.S. copy, and once on the Russian copy. Although we were accustomed to working with the Russian lawyer in Geneva, on this occasion she was glamorously dressed and looked terrific. U.S. social media immediately began asking who is that woman behind Medvedev?

RATIFICATION STARTING GUN

Afterwards, there was a ceremonial lunch and then President Obama was whisked off to other meetings. We were brought outside to a media tent in the castle courtyard. This was the first time the full treaty had seen the light of day, so the press was clamoring for information. We were aware that this press conference was the starting gun for the ratification debate in the U.S. Senate, so we had to get the messages right.

The press questions made it clear that stories had already begun to circulate that this treaty was not as good as START, its predecessor. They were pointed and detailed, touching on technical matters such as telemetry, on-site inspection, and counting rules that would come up again and again on Capitol Hill. I was proud that we managed to perform well under the press fire, getting the word out about the substance of the treaty. Nobody knew it better than we did, and so even in that first encounter, we were able to lay down the right message: every treaty is unique, and so is this one—it does some things better than START, and other things that START did were not needed. New START is different from START, and there are good reasons why.

The tent was plastic and the sun was hot, so by the time the press finished with their questions, we were all sweating. But we were still standing, and the New START Treaty was on its way to ratification.

CHAPTER 12

UP TO THE SENATE

THE FINAL SCRUB

Right after Prague, the delegation family dispersed and headed back to Washington, DC. We had lived and worked so closely together that it seemed impossible that we wouldn't be seeing each other every day, but in truth, everybody was ready to go home. We were missing our real families, and everybody had catching up to do. Most of us had deferred medical care, dental appointments, and haircuts. I had to return to the dentist twice just to get my teeth completely clean—I think they sandblasted them—and I never looked so shaggy as the day when I finally showed up at my hairdresser's. Only the delegation members from the Joint Chiefs of Staff escaped looking unkempt. They all went to the Geneva barber who cut the Marines' hair and came back with their heads shaved.

We had to jump right into getting the treaty package ready to go up to the Senate and begin the ratification process. The treaty must be accompanied by a careful description on an article-by-article basis. We also needed to prepare fact sheets and background material to back up briefings and hearings on Capitol Hill. The Obama Administration was keen to get the treaty through the Senate advice-and-consent process so that the president could ratify it. Since START had ended in December 2009, we and the Russians were left only with the Moscow Treaty, which contained no verification measures of its own. The sooner we got New START into force, the sooner we could resume on-site inspections and other measures to ensure that we knew what the Russians were doing with their nuclear forces, and vice versa.

There were also some political drivers for moving quickly into the ratification process: The Senate and the House in 2010 were both in the hands of Democratic leaders, but with Congressional elections in the offing in the fall, it was not clear how long that advantageous situation would continue. As a Democrat, President Obama would have a more difficult time in any event getting a nuclear treaty through the Senate, but his stance on moving toward zero nuclear weapons in the Prague Initiative had generated further headwinds. As we'd found out during Senator Kyl's visit to Geneva, a number of Republican senators were highly skeptical that Obama would continue to do what was necessary to maintain U.S. strategic forces. Moreover, they were keen to get him to commit to modernizing the nuclear triad.

One loose end had to be dealt with in Geneva, however, and that was a final scrubbing through the technical annexes to make sure that they were identical in Russian and English. The annexes contain all the detailed procedures for conducting inspections and other important treaty implementation measures. They become like a handbook for inspectors, and so they must be accurate in both languages.

Neil Couch and Marshall Brown had stayed behind in Geneva with a small group, including our Russian linguists, to scrub the annexes with their Russian counterparts. Within a few short days, however, they were not getting along well, fighting over every phrase and getting on each other's nerves in general. Looking back, I think that everyone was just tired. After the adrenalin of the signing ceremony had drained away, they simply couldn't stand the sight of each other any longer. The Russians announced that they were leaving to go back to Moscow for a rest—they had bought the tickets and were heading to the airport that very day. They did not say exactly when they would come back, but they indicated it would be a short break.

When I heard about it, I knew there would be trouble because the White House wanted no delay in getting the whole package, annexes included, ready to go up to the Senate. With some trepidation, I sent word of what was happening to my boss, Ellen Tauscher. Within what seemed like seconds, my secretary came in with a worried face. "Undersecretary Tauscher is on the phone," she said, "and she's mad about something."

Tauscher gave me the dressing-down of my life, shouting that she kept saving me from the White House and I kept screwing up. Who told me that I could release the working group in Geneva? They needed to get their work done so we could get the blessed treaty up to the Senate.

Mildly I tried to say that I had not released the group; the Russians had upped and left. I too had had no warning. Tauscher was having none of it. "What are you going to do about it?" she demanded. Thinking fast, I told her that I would call my Russian counterpart in Moscow and see if our team could follow the Russian team to Moscow and get the work done there. "Do it," she said and slammed down the phone.

Eyjafjallajokull to the Rescue

What I had promised wasn't easy because our experts would need to have instant visas issued by the Russians. If the Russians didn't want to see them, they could simply delay the visas for an indefinite period. I called Neil Couch back in Geneva and told him what I was planning to do, and why. He said he and his colleagues would be ready to go. Then I called Antonov in Moscow.

Antonov didn't answer his mobile phone—by that time, it was already long after working hours on a Friday—but his executive secretary, Sergei

Rudenko, did. Rudenko listened to my request and readily agreed to work on the problem. He said he would get instructions to the Russian Mission in Geneva to issue the visas immediately and would speak with the Russian team to ensure that they would be ready to go back to work on Monday. He promised to find the necessary meeting space on the premises of the Ministry of Foreign Affairs and offered to help reserve hotel rooms.

I told him that would not be necessary. My next call was to the U.S. ambassador in Moscow, John Beyrle, to seek his support for the delegation. No official person travels to any country in the world without country clearance from the U.S. ambassador there, and sometimes it can take a while to get this clearance. Beyrle, who is an old friend, was very understanding and said he would issue the clearance immediately. He also asked his staff to help us reserve hotel rooms and transport for the delegation.

So it seemed we were in business: the U.S. team would be able to travel to Moscow over the weekend and go back to work with their Russian counterparts on Monday. What their Russian counterparts would make of the plan I did not know, but I hoped that the combination of Anatoly Antonov and Sergei Rudenko would cajole them back into action.

With this news, I called back Couch and told him that he and his colleagues should pack their bags for Moscow. Then I called back Tauscher to give her the news. "Good," she said, "I won't have to call the White House."

When I hung up, I sat for a moment in my chair. Then the phone rang again. It was Neil Couch, calling again from Geneva. "Rose," he said, "The Russians were on the way to the airport when they got word that the airport is closed. Ash from the Icelandic volcano has closed it down for the foreseeable future. They are coming back to the Russian Mission."

I just started laughing: Eyjafjallajokull to the rescue! The mountain with unpronounceable name had been spewing ash for a few days, and there had been worry about interference with flights over the Atlantic, but I never expected it would close down the Geneva Airport completely. In the end, it closed European airports and disrupted air travel for several weeks—long enough to get the annexes done.

I called Moscow back again and this time managed to get Antonov on the phone, despite the late hour. We both knew the teams were tired because they had been working seven days a week for over a month. After a good laugh about the volcano, we agreed that they should take the weekend off to rest and begin again on Monday morning. I think we even agreed to schedule the meeting in the Russian Mission, and I left it to Antonov to buck up his people to ensure that they would show up for work.

Then I called back Tauscher again. I told her matter-of-factly that because of the airport closure, the Russian experts had not left Geneva after all. They would resume work there with our experts and get the annexes finished in the coming days. I did not tell her that Antonov and I had given them the weekend off.

This third big blow-up over my management of the delegation has led me to do some soul-searching: did I not comprehend the cues coming from the politicians? I knew getting the annexes finished was urgent, but I also understood the heavy fatigue of those who had been working on them. I did not think that a few days of rest would make a big difference to completion of the package, especially because I knew that the article-by-article analysis was still underway and would take some time to complete. I was also confident that the Russians weren't playing with us: they would not delay completion; they just needed a little time back home.

In truth, I am not sure the White House understood the importance as well as the strain of sustained delegation work. It had been twenty years since the last high-intensity nuclear negotiation in Geneva, which had taken close to six years and a delegation of well over a hundred people. Reflecting on my experience at the START talks, I thought we'd done pretty well to get this treaty negotiated in one year with a delegation of seventy people.

The White House certainly did not remember. One day a prominent advisor stopped me when I was on my way into a meeting in the Situation Room. "Do you really need all those people spending months in Geneva?" he asked. "Can't you do this with a small team who goes over there for a couple of weeks?" I didn't say much, other than quietly mentioning all the detailed technical work that goes into putting a treaty together.

In some ways, I think I am too much of a technocrat and maybe too much of a sympathetic boss. I did not comprehend the political cues, and I was thinking about the accuracy of the process and the exhausted people more than the need to get it done. Knowing that the more tired they were, the more they would make mistakes was part of my acceptance of the Russian departure. I obviously should have kicked up a fuss from the first moment—that would have been the right response. Anyway, an act of God saved us. In the end, my inadequate political instincts did not matter.

The Package Comes Together

Once the annexes were scrubbed and the treaty documents were safely together, the article-by-article analysis was finished quickly. That work is carried out by lawyers in the State Department's legal office, which becomes the custodian of a treaty once it is signed. They have a vault where treaties are kept, at least those from recent decades. Once during this period, I went to view the New START Treaty there. The sanctuary was solemn and dark, and as the newest treaty to be signed, New START had a table all to itself. I was a little disappointed that it wasn't surrounded by burning red candles, but it was being treated well enough.

The article-by-article process was a bit of a mystery to many in the arms control interagency, because they had never gone through the ratification process of a treaty. Even the lawyers were not completely familiar with the procedures. Luckily, I had a great asset in Terri Lodge, who had worked in State's Congressional Affairs office and had overseen ratification of ten treaties. She had seen some great victories—the Conventional Forces in Europe Treaty, the Chemical Weapons Convention—but she had also seen some bitter defeats, such as the Comprehensive Test Ban Treaty. She knew exactly the kind of heavy lifting that was going to be needed as well as the importance of having a strong "trail boss" for the process.

Another great asset was Lynn Rusten, who had overseen the backstopping team for the delegation in Geneva and now stepped forward to oversee the interagency process for preparing treaty information, including fact sheets and answers to questions for the record. Her role was vital to maintaining consistency because questions for the record began to come in from individual senators, and not only through the official process led by the Senate Foreign Relations Committee (SFRC) but also through other committees.

The Senate Armed Services Committee and Senate Select Intelligence Committee were especially active, and naturally questions through them went to the Pentagon and the intelligence agencies to answer, not to State Department, where the SFRC questions landed. If each agency were answering its questions without clearing them with other agencies, we could have ended up with a shambolic situation. With support from the White House, Rusten ensured that all questions for the record went through a clearance process. The answers did not need to be identical, but they did need to be consistent.

On May 13, 2010, the New START Treaty went up to the Senate with its article-by-article analysis. It arrived just over one month from the Prague signing on April 8, despite the volcanic eruption getting in the way—record time for a package of its kind. Immediately, we began to set the schedule for hearings. The Cabinet secretaries would go first, beginning with Secretary Clinton, but then those who had worked on the negotiations would have their turn.

Here was where tragedy struck. Ellen Tauscher, who had played an important role in the negotiation endgame and naturally wanted to testify, called me up to her office one day. She calmly told me that she had been diagnosed with cancer and would be taking time off for surgery and treatment. "I haven't been feeling well," she said, "and in particular have been finding it hard to eat, so I need to take care of this." As usual, she was tough but cheerful, already working the details of how to keep up her work while she was absent from the Department. I admired her calm and told her we would miss her savvy on Capitol Hill. Right away she said that she would be keeping up the pressure even from her hospital bed—and she did.

So I had the lead to testify on the State Department's behalf once Secretary Clinton had finished her hearing. As it turned out, the same people who had led in Geneva—Ted Warner, Mike Elliott, Dick Trout, Kurt Siemon, and I—continued to play a significant role throughout the ratification process. As we knew from our first press conference in Prague, we were the ones who knew the treaty inside and out, and we could articulate the rationale for why things had been negotiated in a particular way. Our "insiders' view" was vital, but we were joined by a couple of heavy hitters who had the political clout to wheel and deal on Capitol Hill, especially James Miller and Sandy Winnefeld from the Defense Department. James Clapper, the director for National Intelligence, joined in late and played a critical role in the final ratification vote.

President Obama was clearly paying a lot of attention to the success of this treaty because he asked Vice President Joe Biden to take the lead on the ratification process—a "trail boss" of top caliber. I believe that this decision was crucial. It ensured that the highest level of attention went to issues that needed to be resolved quickly, such as what kind of budget funds could be made available for nuclear modernization.

The vast experience of Vice President Biden in the Senate was another highly necessary commodity. The senators on both sides of the aisle were his longtime colleagues, and he made good use of his capacity to cajole and charm—and make deals. I appreciated his willingness to put a lot of personal capital into the process, inviting senators to his office either just off the Senate floor or in the White House and to the Roosevelt Room in the West Wing.

Vice President Biden also supplied us with a secret weapon—Brian McKeon, his highly experienced deputy national security advisor, who knew and understood the ratification process. A knowledgeable lawyer, McKeon was well equipped to deal with the delicate negotiations over a resolution of ratification for the treaty. Although he never let on, he probably knew the quirks of every staffer who would work on the treaty, and he also knew their bosses—a great advantage in navigating the tough issues that would arise.

And arise they did. Already during the visit of Senators Feinstein and Kyl to Geneva, we had heard about the need to modernize the nuclear triad, including the funds that the Department of Energy would need for fissile materials and warhead pit production. The senators had also underscored the need for telemetry measures in the treaty, and now they wanted to know why the New START telemetry regime was different from START. Missile defense figured prominently, with loud concerns from some senators that the treaty may contain secret measures to constrain U.S. deployment of missile defenses. And the verification regime was always front and center as a focal point for questions, most of which began with, "Why is this treaty different from START?"

Another set of questions emerged around whether the Russians were up to something in the secret development of new nuclear weapon systems. I can say that in 2010, we had no evidence that the Russians were developing and preparing to deploy the ground-launched intermediate-range cruise missile that later became a clear violation of the INF Treaty. Its nature as a ground-launched system only became clear in 2011, after New START entered into force. Likewise, the new systems that President Putin advertised in his famous speech of March 2018 were either clearly accountable under the treaty—for example, the Sarmat heavy ICBM—or would not be ready for deployment during the life of the treaty.

Since we were intent on negotiating another treaty after New START had entered into force, we believed that we would have ample opportunity to work such issues. Even absent a new negotiation, we knew that New START provided the mechanism for us to question the Russians about any new kinds of weapons that they might develop during the life of the treaty. Those conversations would happen in the Bilateral Consultative Commission (BCC). If we raised questions in the BCC about new weapons, the Russians would have to address them.

The summer passed in a welter of hearings—my first was before the Senate Foreign Relations Committee in July. Many, many briefings also took place to the Senate Armed Services Committee, the Senate Select Committee on Intelligence, the National Security Working Group, and to individual senators and staffers. I remember it being a hot and sticky few months. We would thread our way sweating through construction and security into the Senate side of the Capitol. Expert staff in tow and carrying heavy briefing books, we would have a few hours of grilling before escaping exhausted into the heat again.

All in all, the New START Treaty had over twenty formal hearings and briefings during its ratification process, and each of them generated a new round of questions for the record, or "QFRs" for shorthand. In the end, we answered well more than a thousand QFRs. That is why I was so grateful that Lynn Rusten and her team were riding herd on them. Keeping them organized was no mean feat in its own right, but making sure they were cleared and consistent was a herculean task.

New START's Public Face

The summer was also the time when we began to build public support for the treaty. Here Terri Lodge's long experience in ratification fights was all-important. She advised that support for the treaty in Senate offices could come from unexpected directions, but we needed to take the time to develop the public support to make that happen.

We started with religious organizations and leaders. I grew up a Catholic, so it was not difficult for me to work with the American bishops —specifically, the United States Conference of Catholic Bishops, which has an efficient lobbying organization based near Catholic University in Washington, DC. It was interesting to learn that for these bishops, controlling nuclear weapons is in the same moral realm as the fight against abortion and capital punishment. Anything that causes unwarranted loss of life, I learned, is a cause that Catholics should fight. I briefed the bishops a number of times that summer, either as a group or individually, taking some quick trips to do so.

We also began working with Protestant organizations; the Evangelical movement, at least a sector of it, was very supportive of nuclear disarmament. Many of the religious leaders had not been asked to think about the matter for a long time—since the "freeze movement" of the 1980s and 1990s—but their muscle memory and church policies were in place and ready to again be turned to the purpose of supporting a nuclear disarmament treaty. They became strong advocates for New START.

A trip to Utah brought a surprise, however. I was hoping that the Church of Latter-Day Saints would be supportive because there is a considerable Mormon caucus in Congress. However, the Mormons had gotten caught up in that very freeze movement thirty years prior. The "race-track" mobile MX missile system had been planned for deployment on territory in Utah, and the church leadership had been divided about whether to support it. They faced a great deal of opposition from ranchers and other locals who did not want mobile missiles in their backyard— or on their ranch lands. When Washington suddenly cancelled the MX program because of costs, the Mormon leaders concluded that they had burned a lot of capital for no good purpose and vowed to stay out of nuclear weapon issues in future. That policy held during the ratification of New START, and it holds to this day.

Nonetheless, by the end of summer we had built a great deal of support among religious groups, and they were steady allies throughout the process. They delivered results, working down to the level of local parishes and churches, and in some cases getting individual clergy to weigh in. In one case, a senator's Methodist minister urged him to vote in favor of the treaty, and he did. The long-standing peace organizations supported by the churches were especially enthusiastic allies and put into place tried-and-true tactics for generating buzz on Capitol Hill, particularly campaigns of postcards, letters, and calls from church members around the country.

As fall began, we had shifted into maximum campaign mode. When the Washington elite returned from August vacations, we were ready for them.

CHAPTER 13

THE LAST VOTES

BUILDING SUPPORT ONE BRICK AT A TIME

One of the most basic rules for garnering support in Washington is to get as many names onto a public statement as possible. Ex-presidents, national security advisors, Cabinet secretaries, and senior military officers—the more, the better. And the more the group is bipartisan, the bigger the signal to Capitol Hill that there could be political costs for ignoring or opposing the issue. When September rolled around, we were focused on getting such a high-level statement for New START.

Luckily, we had some immediate help from "The Four Horsemen"— George Shultz, Bill Perry, Henry Kissinger, and Sam Nunn, who in 2007 had signed a seminal opinion piece in the *Wall Street Journal,* calling for the elimination of nuclear weapons. I briefed each of them about the treaty—Shultz and Perry on the telephone at Stanford, and Nunn at his law offices in Washington, DC, but Henry Kissinger summoned me to New York. Once again, I rode the train to New York in trepidation and underwent a severe cross-examination. He left me wondering if the treaty would have his support, but within a few days the word came back: The Four Horsemen would lend their support to its ratification.

With them headlining the statement, we rather quickly were able to gain a number of prominent retired leaders on both sides of the aisle, but some wanted to be briefed in person before they would decide. Colin Powell was one of these. The Obama team, keen to have him on board, invited him in to meet with senior figures at the White House. After those discussions, he and I sat down in one of the small briefing spaces in the Situation Room and he grilled me for a good half-hour about the ins and outs of the treaty. He too left without showing his cards, but following a phone conversation with Michael Mullen, we found out we had him on board.

It was more difficult to gain the support of the presidents. Jimmy Carter and Bill Clinton were ready to do so from the outset, but we were hoping to get George H.W. Bush and George W. Bush on board too. To accomplish that goal, I had started even during the negotiations to brief James Baker, the influential secretary of state during the George H.W. Bush administration. When I continued the process during the fall, he had many difficult questions for me, but it was clear he was taking the matter seriously.

We reached out to a number of experienced advisors to the Bush family and other Republican leaders, briefing them quietly in their offices in Washington, DC, or over the telephone. I especially wanted to speak with President Ronald Reagan's chief of staff, Howard Baker, who had been such a great supporter of U.S. efforts to deal with the breakup of the Soviet nuclear arsenal in the 1990s. Despite skepticism elsewhere in his party, he fully supported our efforts to make sure that Russian fissile material and warheads did not fall into the hands of terrorists.

Sadly, Howard Baker had fallen ill, but I spoke by phone with Nancy Kassebaum, his wife and an influential politician in her own right, a former senator from Kansas. She was extremely kind to me, and we remembered together a visit that I had made to their home in Tennessee, when Baker had regaled us with tales about the origins of the Manhattan Project at Oak Ridge. He was an incredible raconteur. She promised to do what she could to support the treaty and to speak to him about it. They both lent their names to the statement.

I got together quietly with anyone who would meet with me, or talked with them on the phone, and I also did many public events. Everyone on the team was engaged in this effort, and I knew I could always get help when I needed it from my colleagues or seniors and betters. The signatures kept growing on the New START statement, and they had a definite bipartisan edge, which was a great feeling. We did not know until the very end, however, if the Bush family would support it. Two weeks before the treaty was up for a vote in the Senate, George H.W. Bush issued a statement saying that it was worthy of support. Finally! That was a huge moment.

The media was another target that we focused on increasingly as winter came on. In New York, I met with the *Wall Street Journal* editorial board to try to temper their skepticism about the treaty. It was another hard meeting, but I was glad that they were making the effort to really learn about the details. Afterwards, I thought that their coverage of New START became more temperate—although maybe I was just imagining it.

Just as important was a trip that I took to Iowa to meet with the editorial board of the *Des Moines Register*. This newspaper, long known for its sophisticated election coverage, also paid attention to national security issues. Their articles were picked up by a number of newspapers in their syndicate across the Midwest and Rocky Mountain states. If we could get them to write a favorable editorial and endorse ratification of New START, then that would get more information about the treaty to people in those states. In turn, that would help our campaign get more letters and cards supporting the treaty into offices on Capitol Hill.

When I went into the Des Moines headquarters, it was evident that I was stepping into a fine newspaper tradition. Several awards, including Pulitzers, were on display, as were many, many photos of politicians who had come to pay tribute to the Iowa caucuses. The editorial board members were no-nonsense newspaper veterans with a keen nose for nonsense. They were by no means pushovers on New START, and I spent over an hour going through the treaty's benefits to U.S. national security as well as its technical details. They had clearly internalized the critiques of the verification regime that were out in the media, and they wanted to know what I had to say about them. Again, I did not know that I had succeeded in convincing them until I saw their editorial some days later.

The broadcast media were also constant and picked up pace as the fall wore on. One that sticks in my head was a Sunday morning talk show for C-SPAN that had a big call-in component to it. We figured it would be a good way to answer questions about the treaty from a wide audience. The questions were indeed all over the map, but only one came close to stumping me. One caller from Virginia asked me if the treaty would in any way impact his Second Amendment rights. After all, it was about arms control, wasn't it? He was sincerely concerned.

I was tempted to say that unless he had an ICBM in his back yard, he shouldn't be worried, but I thought better of it. Instead, I said simply that the treaty was about nuclear weapons and in no way touched on his right to bear arms. To this day, I'm not sure I convinced him.

While these new efforts went on, we continued to work hard with the groups who had supported us from the outset, including advocacy groups such as the Arms Control Association. It's funny when I look back on it, but at the time, the groups were not particularly excited about the New START Treaty, nor were they particularly complimentary. President Obama had promised additional deep cuts during his time in office, in line with his Prague speech, and this treaty, as they saw it, was only a quick-fix interim measure until we could get to that more ambitious treaty. The treaty was a bit of a nothing-burger, in their words, but they would support it as a necessary first step.

To their credit, the advocacy groups threw themselves fully behind the ratification process and did important work to generate the campaign that began to inundate Senate offices with cards and letters. They also were a multiplier for getting information out about the treaty, working constantly with the media, and doing countless interviews and information sessions. They worked in close coordination with the religious organizations, who continued to be our strong allies.

Indeed, some of the most active advocacy groups, such as the Friends Committee on National Legislation, were offspring of religious organizations, in this case the Quakers. The group's experienced director, David Culp, was one of the wisest heads in Washington on Senate politics. I turned to him not only for advice but also for his whip count on the treaty. He helped to nurture the Republican votes that were beginning to take shape, linking up with Senate staff and getting them information— or getting me to talk to them when it was necessary.

When the vote was coming soon, we organized a memorable phone call with the religious groups who were working to build support for the treaty. There must have been close to fifty people on the call, and my job was to answer their questions and give them a sense of priorities in the endgame of the ratification process.

When I opened the call to their questions, the first person who spoke said, "Hello, this is your cousin Doris." I was stunned. Sister Doris Gottemoeller and I had spent our careers in very different orbits. She, a Mercy sister, had essentially been the CEO of a large Catholic hospital network in the United States. I had always looked up to her, but she was the last person whom I expected to hear on a call about an arms control treaty. "I just wanted to let you know that the religious women of America are supporting everything you're doing," she said, "And praying for you." That was wonderful to hear, I told her, the best help I could get.

RESOLUTION OF RATIFICATION (ROR)

As December arrived, we were deep in negotiation of the Resolution of Ratification (ROR) for the New START Treaty. The "ROR," as we called it, is an important document. While their vote expresses the consent of the Senate to the treaty, the ROR expresses their advice about it—and both advice and consent are inscribed in the Constitution as the role of the Senate in the ratification process.

Luckily, we had Brian McKeon to lead the negotiations. As a lawyer and former Senate staffer, he knew all the tricks likely to be thrown at us. As Vice President Biden's representative, he also carried the full weight of the White House at the table. Terri Lodge, who had negotiated ten RORs, was my experienced hand—a good thing because I had never negotiated even one. Her knowledge came in very handy to find compromises that would answer the senators' requirements without locking us in on certain demands. It was critical that we avoid changing the treaty through the process of ROR negotiation. If we did somehow impact the treaty's legal meaning, then the Russians could refuse to ratify it themselves, and it would never enter into force.

On the Senate side, we also had extremely experienced staffers—Edward Levine and Anthony Wier (working for Senator Kerry, the chairman of the Senate Foreign Relations Committee) as well as Stacy Oliver (working for the ranking minority member, Senator Bob Corker). Senator Lugar's staff—especially Kenneth Myers, the equivalent of a staff elder statesman who had been through many ratification battles—were also critical. And although he could not sit in on every meeting, we knew that we needed to hear firsthand from Senator Kyl's staffer, Tim Morrison. Senator Kyl and his focus on nuclear modernization had to be taken into account.

Senators could suggest and, in some cases, would demand language that they wanted to see in the resolution. In the New START case, Senator Kyl made sure that modernization was front and center. He wanted to ensure that if the treaty were to pass, then the Administration would provide funding to modernize the nuclear triad. A number of senators focused on missile defense—they wanted to make sure that no part of the treaty or its underlying documents did anything to constrain missile defenses. There was a persistent rumor around Capitol Hill that somehow we had a negotiated a "secret deal" to limit defenses, and the senators wanted to be certain that no such thing could happen. Some other highly technical issues played into the ROR, but those were the main substantive points.

A cold bright sun reigned in Washington, DC, those days, but I was rushing around town sweating. It seemed to me the entire team never stopped running. One day I had to brief a session in Herndon, at an intelligence conference, and then rush down to Capitol Hill to work on the ROR negotiations. Since it was after rush hour, I figured I could make it in an hour, but an immense traffic jam kept me on the road for over two hours.

I finally roared down First Street and left my car as close as I dared to the Russell Senate Office Building, in a blatantly illegal spot. I ran all the way to the SFRC offices and arrived panting to the glares of Brian McKeon, Terri Lodge, and the Senate staffers. They had just gotten to the part about missile defenses, so it was good timing, but I was glad that I didn't have a heart attack on the way. We got the draft ROR finished that day, and when I left the building a few hours later, I thought to myself, "If my car has not been towed, then this treaty is going to pass the Senate." My car was where I left it, and I didn't even get a ticket.

THE CAMP ON CAPITOL HILL

In the second week of December, we decided we needed to set up camp in the Senate wing of the Capitol, so that we would be constantly available to senators and their staff. We set up in the formal hearing room for the Senate Foreign Relations Committee, a beautiful and historic space. It had an enormous oval table and chairs, with more chairs set around the wall. The chatelaine of the space, Meg Murphy, arranged to have a large and heavy cardboard cover put on the table to protect it from our many briefing books, but she insisted that no food or drink could be brought into the room. That lasted about one day because we were working until at least 11:00 p.m. every night and never leaving the Capitol. We had to grab food, and, most importantly, coffee from wherever we could get it. Murphy, to her great credit, turned a blind eye.

Brian McKeon took over the vice president's office off the Senate floor, also a beautiful space, small but with windows looking out over the Capitol grounds, and wonderfully decorated for Christmas. It had a working fireplace and McKeon kept a fire burning, which eventually curled the poinsettias but was welcome to the rest of us. It was still very cold outside, and when we left in the middle of the night, the stars were hard and clear and the temperature below freezing.

It was in that office that we planned the last meetings and briefings that we needed to do. Ted Warner, Mike Elliott, and I were part of a team that made repeated visits to Republican Senate offices to talk to members and staff as well as to the Senate secure facility, the SCIF, to brief on classified questions. Sometimes we were joined by James Miller and Sandy Winnefeld, when special messages needed to be delivered from SecDef, or from Admiral Mullen.

James Miller was deft at talking with senators and canny at delivering messages they needed to hear. When Senator Lisa Murkowski of Alaska asked him if it would be possible for the Administration to consider opening up an additional field for missile defense interceptors in Alaska, he was ready with an answer: yes. I admired how well prepared he was with that simple answer. From the State Department, I would not have found it possible.

Another senior figure who made himself available for the endgame was James Clapper, the director of National Intelligence and most senior figure in the intelligence establishment. He lent great authority to the answers that we had been giving about the status of Russian missile developments, backing up the many briefings that we had given. He did not particularly like sitting in the vice president's Senate office with the rest of us, however, and I don't blame him. It was not always possible to know with precision when senators would be available, and that is why we were staying close to the Senate floor: we could grab them as they came off it for ad hoc meetings. Clapper, I am sure, was not used to waiting.

But Clapper was of great help in talking with Senator Joe Manchin, Democrat from West Virginia. Senator Manchin had recently arrived in the Senate, and his views on foreign policy were unknown. Two things were clear, however: West Virginia is a conservative state and usually leans Republican, and the White House wanted every single Democrat to vote for the New START Treaty if it was humanly possible.

We knew from talking to Senator Manchin's staff that he wanted to understand more about the intelligence that he had been reading, so we asked him to meet with Clapper in the vice president's office. When Senator Manchin arrived at last from the Senate floor, we sat down around the table and Clapper asked him about his concerns. It was a serious and detailed conversation, and I was impressed that the new senator from West Virginia was so thoroughly briefed on the treaty.

Senator Manchin was also very clear about his own political environment, making note that his was a conservative state not used to seeing their senator vote with the Democrats. He wanted to know how the votes were shaping up, and Brian McKeon was able to confirm that several senators from the Republican side had already confirmed their willingness to vote in favor. He went away indicating that he was leaning to a positive vote too, which his office later confirmed. We thanked Clapper profusely and he said, "I hope it was worth it."

As the last days of the session approached, we were still on the hunt for two Republican votes, and they were both from Arizona: Senator Jon Kyl and Senator John McCain. Kyl had been following the negotiations from the outset, had come to Geneva with Dianne Feinstein, and had made clear his price for a positive vote: President Obama needed to agree to a modernization of the nuclear triad, and he needed to ensure that his budget provided for it.

The president had a well-articulated position that as long as nuclear weapons exist, the United States must have a safe, secure, and effective arsenal, and so the administration already had a rationale to modernize within the logic of the Prague initiative. However, Senator Kyl and some other Republicans doubted that he would actually go forward with modernization, so they insisted that the money be on the table as well. These were issues that not only were worked out through months of discussion in the ratification process but were also inscribed in the Resolution of Ratification. Senator Kyl got what he wanted.

So it was much to our surprise when he went to the Senate floor and declared that he could not possibly vote for the treaty. We were stunned: after all that effort, all those dollars agreed to in the budget? It is not unusual for a national security issue to be treated transactionally in the Senate, but the White House had taken Senator Kyl's concerns seriously and met his financial benchmarks. His last-minute declaration was greeted with disbelief, and not only among Democrats. In my opinion, his last-minute change of heart was seen as bad faith on both sides of the aisle. It contributed to Republican willingness to let the treaty come to the floor for a vote.

Senator McCain was a different matter. An eminent figure on defense and national security matters and ranking member of the Senate Armed Services Committee, he was someone who should have, we felt, been willing to vote in favor of the treaty. Senator Kerry, the Foreign Relations chairman, felt he was eminently "gettable." But Senator McCain also had very strong views about the issue of gays in the military, which was concurrently on the Senate floor with the New START Treaty. He did not like what the Obama administration was doing to move beyond President Clinton's "don't ask, don't tell" policy. In fact, Senator McCain was furious about it.

Chairman Kerry asked me to join him in his office next to the Senate floor for a late-night meeting with Senator McCain, and to my surprise, this issue was front and center. Kerry and I tried to talk to him about the value of the treaty, and the importance of his vote, and he just got madder. He declared he would vote against the treaty to protest against Obama's gays in the military policy, and then he stormed out of the office. Kerry said to me simply, "Let him go. When he gets angry like that, there is nothing that you can do to change his mind."

Anyway, by that time it was becoming clear that we could manage without the two senators from Arizona. Brian McKeon was keeping track of the votes, and we were getting closer, if we could get through the last negotiation on the Resolution of Ratification. We had worked it out at the staff level, but the senators would have the final say.

On December 19, we had an unpleasant surprise, however. Michael Gordon of *The New York Times* had discovered that the negotiating record of the New START Treaty was on Wikileaks, and he had started to comb through the cables. Gordon for many years had been one of the best national security correspondents in the business, and he really knew and understood arms control. There was nothing in the negotiating record that I could not defend, but we had taken a firm position throughout the ratification process against Republican demands to make the negotiating record available to them. Such documents are the protected property of the executive branch, and they are never made available because they record a work in progress, not the final product. The final product is laid out in the article-by-article analysis that the Senate had received in May. How the pudding gets made is the president's business; advice and consent is the Senate's business.

Gordon, however, was very interested in how the pudding had been made and wanted to discuss various details. He called me, he called Ted Warner, he called Mike Elliott, and we all talked to him to try to dissuade him from writing. We were certain that we could defend the negotiating record, but we foresaw his piece leading to a new round of questions, perhaps a new round of hearings, and the vote would get pushed into the unforeseeable future—a dangerous delay, especially with no nuclear arms treaty in force.

At White House instruction, I tried to persuade Gordon that we would give him an exclusive interview when the vote was over, to give him whatever blow-by-blow account interested him. He was having none of it.

So it was with a sense of dread that I woke up on December 20 and looked at *The New York Times.* No Michael Gordon article. December 21, no Michael Gordon article. I didn't know what was happening, but I was afraid to call him, and we weren't hearing anything from the White House press office or anybody else. So I decided to forget about it and hope for the best.

The next week, I called Michael Gordon and asked if he wanted to do the exclusive story we'd offered him. No, he said, his editor wasn't interested any more, the story was already going cold. Anyway, he had just gotten out of the hospital: he had been all ready to press "send" on the story when his back had gone out so badly that his wife had had to call an ambulance. He'd spent almost a week in the hospital, and the story never got done.

People have teased me about this tale, asking if I invoked some kind of voodoo procedure to prevent the article from being published. I can assure the reader that I did not, but like the volcano incident, it seemed to be another act of God, this time involving Michael Gordon.

On December 21, we entered last-minute negotiations with certain senators on the Resolution of Ratification. The issue of missile defense was still bothering them, and they wanted to make absolutely certain that there were no limits on missile defenses hidden in the treaty. They zeroed in on the statement that the Russians had made about missile defenses, focusing on the Russian comment that if the United States built up missile defenses, Russia may review its continuing participation in the New START treaty. Was that some kind of hidden limit?

Late in the afternoon, I got word that Secretary Clinton was coming up to Capitol Hill to take stock of our efforts and lend support by talking to senators if needed. I was briefing Secretary Clinton in the SFRC hearing room when Vice President Biden and Senator Kerry also arrived, carrying the Resolution of Ratification. "What if we use this formulation in the resolution?" Senator Kerry said to me. I took a look at what was being proposed, which would have imposed a new condition on implementation of the treaty. I looked up and both the vice president and the chairman of the SFRC were staring at me intently. I knew that Secretary Clinton was right behind me. I took a deep breath and said, "Mr. Chairman, if you impose this new condition on U.S. implementation of the treaty, then the Russians will not ratify it and it will never enter into force." Then, said Senator Kerry, we will stick with what we have.

I always say that was the worst moment of my professional life, having to stand up to the vice president and the chairman with my boss at my back. There is a great photo that captures the moment because the Senate photographer was recording some of the events of those days (see figure 9). On reflection, maybe it was not the worst moment, but I was certain it could have meant the end of the treaty.

The next day, December 22, was supposed to be the day of the vote, but I was so tired that I had lost track of whether it was actually scheduled. I had not been keeping track of the whip count, but Brian McKeon was. While we were sitting in the vice president's office that morning, where the poinsettias by this time were decidedly dead, he said to me, "You should go ahead and invite your delegation to the vote, it's going to happen this afternoon." "Really?" I said, "how do I get them in?" He told me that the sergeant-at-arms would provide the needed gallery passes and told me to go ahead and start making calls.

"That is very kind of you, Brian," I said, but in truth, I was surprised. No one in the White House had ever shown any interest in my delegation and how hard they had worked. This was the first time that they had received an invitation to bask in the treaty's success. I must say I was touchingly grateful.

In any event, when I arrived in the Senate gallery that afternoon with my husband, both sons, and one of their fiancées, it was packed with the entire delegation from across the interagency—State, Defense, Energy, and intelligence organizations were all there. It was the first time the Geneva family had come together in one place since we'd left there the previous April. I was glad to see them all.

As we waited for the vote, my son Daniel said how much, seen from above, the Senate floor looked like a fish tank. Senators swooped in, descending on colleagues to greet them. The women hugged, the men did the Washington grip, perfected by President Clinton: a handshake, the other hand gripping the arm or elbow of the other, drawing them in close for a personal word. They moved around the floor, repeating the greeting, and it looked to me like it didn't matter whether one was Republican or Democrat, everybody was in on it. Secretary Clinton appeared and, as a former senator, was greeted like a long-lost friend. It was the last day of votes before the Christmas break, and everyone was in a good mood whether they liked the treaty or not.

Vice President Biden took the chair, and the Senate was called to order for the ratification vote on the New START Treaty. I knew we had the votes, so I was not especially nervous, but it was interesting to watch how the senators voiced their "aye" or "no." Senator McCain growled his "no," turning thumbs down, but Senator Kerry, the Chairman of the Senate Foreign Relations Committee, strode down the aisle, perfectly timed to say "aye." His was the sixty-seventh and decisive vote in favor of the treaty. We were across the finish line. In the end, the vote was seventy-two in favor, twenty-seven against, with one senator not voting.

When the vote was called out in favor of the treaty, my delegation in the gallery erupted in cheers and applause, and so did people across the chamber—senators, staffers, the public in the galleries. I watched people who had come at random to the vote, those who had stood in line for a chance to visit the Senate chamber knowing nothing about the New START Treaty. They were thrilled to be there for the vote, no matter what it was about. (See figure 10.)

After it was all over, I was sitting in the Senate corridor, on one of the benches in an ornate window alcove. I was dazed and exhausted, but finally I was beginning to feel that we had managed, somehow, to succeed. A Republican staffer approached me, a man with a lot of savvy as well as vitriol. He looked down at me and said, "You won this one, but I'll get you." Welcome to Washington.

CHAPTER 14

THE GOLD STANDARD TREATY —LESSONS LEARNED

My lessons learned in negotiating the New START Treaty are sometimes painful, sometimes mundane, sometimes delightful. They are delightful in that they remind me of humankind's ability to follow a rough road and laugh along the way. They are mundane because they are found in every management textbook; I don't think I made any brilliant discoveries about how to get the best out of people. They are painful because they highlight my own ignorance or lack of savvy: after forty years in Washington, I did not know everything.

In this chapter, I try to pull all the lessons together, food for thought for future negotiators.

DEFINE YOUR SECURITY OBJECTIVE AND STICK WITH IT

The most important lessons have to do with political imperatives, and first among these is the U.S. national security objective, carefully defined. Some consider an arms control process to be a natural good, to be pursued for its own sake. My view instead is that negotiations are a waste of time unless they serve U.S. national security. In New START, as in its predecessor agreement, we defined the U.S. national security objective as reducing and eliminating Russian strategic offensive nuclear forces that are an existential threat to the United States. In doing so, we ensured that the Russians cannot break out quickly to deploy bigger numbers, and we created a monitoring system that guarantees we will know if they fail to comply with the treaty.

This objective seemed to suit the Russian side too because when President Obama and President Medvedev first got together in London in April 2009, they agreed fairly readily that the new treaty would be about reducing strategic offensive forces. It truly helped that we, the negotiators, had that goal defined early. It was then backed up by more detailed negotiating instructions that the presidents issued when they met in Moscow in July of that year.

If that message had been unclear, we'd have been mired in endless wrangling over placing constraints on strategic missile defenses. In my opinion, the treaty would never have been finished and signed, much less presented to the Senate for ratification. So, some in the Russian system —including the important prime minister, Vladimir Putin—had to put up with an objective that they did not fully embrace. It is to his credit that Putin later came to consider New START the "gold standard" of strategic arms reduction treaties and to argue unconditionally for its extension.

So, in my view, national security objectives articulated at the highest level as early as possible in the process are essential. Such early embrace means that the leaders are interested enough to stay engaged throughout the negotiations, which is a huge boon to the negotiating teams, even if this is sometimes difficult to deal with.

If the presidents are interested, then so is the rest of the government— another huge boon to the negotiators. The fact that the chairman of the Joint Chiefs of Staff, Admiral Mullen, was willing to give his time on two occasions, once to travel to Geneva and once to Moscow, is a tribute to the benefit of high-level engagement, which began with President

Obama. The whole government set it as a priority, including its highest level of military, civilian, and political players. That engagement, in turn, helps build momentum and solve problems quickly.

THE DARK SIDE

At the same time, the dark side of high-level engagement needs to be understood. I learned patience when high-level interlocutors were yelling at me or fixing me with a baleful stare in White House meetings, including secure videoconferences, the antediluvian version of Zoom. The video conferences between the delegation's secure facility and the White House Situation Room were some of the most painful meetings of my career. I kept bucking myself up with the idea that they did not really want me to quit—probably. My senior colleagues in Geneva were not so sure—they told me that they thought I would be thrown under the bus.

Maybe I was too positive in my meetings with Washington. I am more of a technocrat than a politician, and I felt that the delegation and I could say, "We've got this." Was I being too "smiley," conveying a Pollyannaish optimism rather than a hard-nosed reality? I didn't think so, at the time. Other women negotiators I've known have cultivated a rough and tough demeanor. Maybe I should have too—but I have never been that way, and it doesn't come naturally.

I came to conclude that better communications with Washington at a high level were my responsibility and that I should have been better at it. That is one of the painful lessons I learned from the negotiations. I came into the administration at the last minute, after three years away in Moscow, and I did not have the same wealth of contacts and relationships that others had developed from working on President Obama's campaign.

I am not making excuses. It was a problem that I should have spotted early and made more effort in mitigating. Those at high levels in Washington have a lot on their plates, and they do not like to be surprised. I needed to embrace "no surprises" as dogma, even if I had trouble sometimes figuring out how to get messages to the people who needed to hear them.

It is also important, though, to find a balance: to get as much done as humanly possible without bothering high-level people *because* they have so much on their plates. They didn't want to hear about telemetry *again*. With that difficult issue, we hit a sweet spot when we finally got the right technical people to the table, bringing top experts from Washington and browbeating the Russians into paying attention. To my mind, that was the most important output of the presidential engagement on telemetry. The fact that Presidents Obama and Medvedev talked about it so often finally convinced the Russian Ministry of Defense that the issue would not go away, and they had to find some way to address it.

DEALING WITH THE RUSSIANS

Dealing with the Russians proved to be the most predictable part of the negotiations, but it's worth repeating the lessons of that experience. The Russians have their own political imperatives, and you have to try to see their side of the equation if you are going to get the treaty finished. Seeing their side doesn't mean that you have to succumb to their position. I knew that our Russian counterparts were under a lot of pressure from Putin to insert missile defense constraints into the treaty, but that did not mean we did so. We found ways to give them something on the issue without constraining our program—preambular language that was not legally binding, an exchange of statements, a few other tidbits. These provided enough political satisfaction where it was needed in Moscow.

You also have to think about how to package trades, so that we demand enough in order to then give something on our side. My colleagues such as Kurt Siemon, who had a lot of negotiating experience, were very good about thinking ahead on the most detailed packages, even for such seemingly small details as definitions. Small details can stall progress, and Kurt was very good at presenting balanced packages for which the

Russians could immediately see the logic. It got them to say yes quickly because they recognized that we accepted the need for mutual benefit. This strong, confidence-building behavior contributed greatly to the fast momentum that developed in the negotiations.

We were lucky that we were on the same time scale in New START, agreed at the very outset by Presidents Obama and Medvedev. The Russians are famously skilled at slow-rolling. Soviet Premier Nikita Khrushchev used to brag that he could tell his foreign minister, Andrei Gromyko, to sit on a block of ice for as long as necessary for the other side to capitulate. In New START, however, we both agreed that we had to work as hard and fast as possible to bring a new treaty to fruition before START went out of force in December 2009. It almost worked; if it had not been for Putin's last-minute meddling, we might have made it.

I had to convince older members of my delegation, however, that 2009 was not 1990. We did not need to be constantly scared that the Russians were trying to get the better of us. They like to play games, but not always. We did not need to think that every scheduling attempt was an opportunity for them to try to take advantage of things. Unlike 1990, they *would* pick up the phone when we called; they too had a president breathing down their necks.

Likewise, although it cost me with Washington, I did not think their trips back to Moscow were for purposes of delay or obfuscation. Sometimes they just needed to consult their bosses in the Ministry of Defense or Foreign Affairs. Sometimes, especially at holidays, they were desperate to see their families. So were we.

This need to touch base back home was especially the case because they did not have the use of email for official business. They sent daily reporting cables back to Moscow, but it was never clear to me that the reports were regularly distributed throughout the Russian interagency. So our military counterparts in particular needed to get back from time to time to consult with their bosses—if they wanted to keep their jobs and get the next promotion. This was no joke during that period, which was one of extensive reform in the Ministry of Defense. Many jobs were being cut, including at the general officer level.

On the flip side, I had a lot of fun playing games with them, especially in disturbing the misogyny on the Russian side of the table. I enjoyed sending little gifts at Christmas and Carnival to the women on the Russian delegation, and I enjoyed hearing about it from the men who wondered where their gifts were. I also enjoyed saying to my counterpart that the Russian women should be brought from the backbench to the table and be allowed to speak. Aside from the very capable Russian female interpreters, no woman was ever at the table during the first months of the negotiations. I like to think that my nagging finally brought a Russian expert, a top-notch woman lawyer, to the table for a speaking role.

One last thing I'll say about the Russians: it helps if at least a couple of people on the U.S. delegation speak their language. It doesn't have to be the chief negotiator who speaks Russian—just a good array of diplomats and experts on the U.S. side. Many people on the Russian delegation speak English, some better than I do, and it gives them an advantage. They can listen twice—first to our original presentation and then to the interpretation. This really speeds comprehension and helps minimize misunderstandings.

I had the great benefit of some excellent Russian speakers on the U.S. delegation, and my own Russian-language skills came in handy. I was able to work closely with my counterpart on some of the stickiest issues in the treaty text, ranging freely between English and Russian as we sought to understand each other. We made good use of excellent notetakers from our delegations, who were bilingual on both the U.S. and Russian sides.

No Drive-By Negotiations

It seems obvious but it bears reiterating that negotiating a nuclear arms control treaty cannot be done on a drive-by basis. A two-day visit to Vienna or Geneva is not going to do it. You need sustained effort over a long period of time, by a dedicated delegation that stays in place to keep it up. As my colleague James Timbie has said, "Arms agreements are the result of hard work by people on a mission." Our New START delegation was certainly on a mission.

Our team spanned the U.S. government—State, Defense, Energy, and the intelligence organizations. It also included a number of people from the national nuclear laboratories who brought special knowledge and understanding of some key technical issues. Telemetry is the most prominent example.

Each organization offered up different kinds of expertise. From the State Department came not only diplomats but also lawyers and language specialists as well as the interpreters and translators so important to the negotiations. From DOD came weapon systems operators who knew both the Navy's submarines and the Air Force's bombers and missiles. From the Department of Energy and the laboratories came nuclear warhead experts and those who understood the details of verification. We needed them all to guide us on technical matters such as radiation detection. From both DOD and the intelligence agencies came experienced inspectors, who knew what had worked and what had not in previous nuclear arms control regimes. They already understood the layout of Russian nuclear bases and how to make the most of the time that would be available on inspections.

At its heart the work was interdisciplinary, and so were the delegation members who came from many diverse backgrounds. Melding it into a coherent team that could produce results for the United States took time and perseverance. It required the support of their organizations to keep them in Geneva and the dedication of the individuals themselves. They had to be ready to spend months without their families, working late nights and into the weekends. They became, indeed, people on a mission.

THE MANAGEMENT PIECE

Running the delegation was a challenge, although I can't say it was worse than others I've encountered. I had just come from three years of managing a fissiparous group at the Carnegie Moscow Center: Russians of all sorts—academics, working class people, prima donnas—and research fellows from across the globe, who arrived to spend a few days or a few months in Moscow. The external pressures of constant surveillance and investigation also weighed heavily. I had to deal with bomb threats against the Carnegie Moscow Center as well as death threats against my researchers.

So the U.S. New START delegation was a relief in that I had only Americans to deal with—but what a variety! Military men, diplomats, intelligence types, technical experts, all put together in a pressure cooker from which there was no escaping. The tight schedule was a constant presence. The Department of Defense had deep enough pockets to cycle people in and out on a regular basis but, after a while, I urged the DOD to minimize the changes because we needed experienced hands who were already steeped in the action.

As in Moscow, we on the U.S. side also had external pressures to confront. They posed constant danger for the members who were concerned about what they would return to when the negotiations were over. They did not want their participation in the New START negotiations to ruin the rest of their careers in their home agencies. As it was, we had our share of physical illness and mental strain. Everybody was missing families and loved ones. I had to pay close attention to modulating tensions not only with Washington but also within the delegation. Otherwise, the whole enterprise could have imploded.

My most basic approach was to keep in touch via a daily all-hands staff meeting. Even though everybody knew when Washington had yelled at me the night before, I never let it change my demeanor at those meetings. I always started out reminding them of the major mission we were on and treated pressures from Washington as strictly the result of the high-level priority placed on our work. I reviewed discussions from the day before, asking each team lead to summarize what they had accomplished and to tell us where there were roadblocks. We decided together what had to go on the agenda for meetings with my counterpart and what could be handled by more effort in the working groups or by the team leads.

When Washington decided to take a more direct role, I also insisted that this would be good for the negotiations. It was nothing to be worried about, I kept saying, although the delegation tended to treat such interventions as proof of our failures. I had to remind them of the long tradition of senior-level people helping to get treaties over the finish line. Indeed, it was a sign of impending success. This argument tended to be cold comfort to the delegation.

We didn't communicate only once a day, but many times. We were all sitting along a single corridor on the third floor of the U.S. Mission in Geneva, and I would drop by the different teams to talk to them about problems or check up on ideas. People regularly came to see me. And we were regularly in the secure facility when we needed to discuss classified material. A constant stream of emails filled in the cracks.

I did my best to maintain a standard of courtesy, not swearing, and not criticizing people either behind their backs or in public. I did not wholly succeed because nerves became so raw that if I somehow spoke differently about someone from one day to the next, or failed to mention somebody in a meeting, it was taken as a slight.

Moreover, other people swore like sailors when I wasn't there. When I went to Copenhagen to participate in the meeting between Presidents Obama and Medvedev, I returned to find that the place had practically melted down over profane outbursts. It was a good thing we were all going home for Christmas and would have a chance to calm down, rest, and recharge. Otherwise, I might have had a delegation in collapse.

The most important work that I did was to pay close attention to morale. With people so far away from home, we did our best to make the holidays—Thanksgiving and Easter—special. Luckily, people were sociable and always ready to help organize a party.

They were also up for various challenges. A haiku competition was popular and produced some pretty good verse. The linguists turned out to be especially deft at haiku. The Joint Staff and the lawyers organized a crawl to various late-night Geneva kebab stands, which were often their only source of sustenance if working late. Star Kebab was the hands-down favorite, although somebody pointed out that the spelling of "star" in Cyrillic looks like "crap."

And then there were the bear and the rubber pig. The pig had his home in the Joint Staff offices and was there as a constant reminder that we did not want to be putting lipstick on any pigs. The bear lived with the lawyers and had to be kept locked in a safe drawer because otherwise he would get up to tricks. Making off with liquor left over from parties was his specialty. He developed a bad drinking habit. Mascots among grown-ups may seem silly, but they kept everybody laughing, an absolute necessity.

We also got together as often as we could after hours, whether for pizza and beer at a café, or cooking dinner for each other (at least those of us who had kitchens). I really enjoyed one Sunday evening when I went to have chili with members of the Joint Chiefs of Staff team. All of them were former bomber or missile guys, and they used to get together on Sundays to cook meals and try to catch some of the U.S. football games that were on that day—despite the six-hour time difference.

This particular Sunday, however, they were watching *Dr. Strangelove*, the bizarre comedy about nuclear war from the early 1960s. I've seen *Dr. Strangelove* many times, but never like this. These guys knew the dialogue by heart and could deliver the lines along with the actors on screen. They also knew when Peter Sellers was cracking up with laughter and ad libbing: I had never noticed before! It was a great evening, and

I think they appreciated that I showed up to eat chili and drink beer. I was the only woman in the room.

Indeed, as the first woman to be chief negotiator of a strategic nuclear arms treaty, I often get asked what was different about my style, what did I do differently from the men? Where morale is concerned, I don't think that I acted differently from any other leader I have known. When I was serving on the START delegation in 1990, I remember clearly that chief negotiator Linton Brooks and his wonderful wife Barbara went out of their way to make sure that the delegation had good opportunities to get together, including at their apartment.

Perhaps the only differences I could point to are my scant regard for protocol and my extra patience. I could either sit at home on a Sunday evening or have chili with the guys from the Joint Chiefs of Staff. With patience, I could keep repeating the same positive mantras forever, never mentioning my sleepless nights and tensions with Washington. I kept up the optimism, no matter what. At the end of the day, the delegation can judge for themselves whether it was different having a woman at the helm.

WORKING THE SENATE

In May 2010, when we sent the New START Treaty to the Senate for advice and consent, I assumed that every senator would vote for the treaty if they were convinced of its national security value and got their questions answered. After all, one of the constitutional responsibilities of the Senate is to give advice and consent to the ratification of treaties; once two-thirds of the Senate or sixty-seven votes are in favor, then the president can complete its ratification and bring the treaty into force.

Nowadays senators are often boxed in by their leaders' insistence on party-line votes, so New START ratification is perhaps less possible today than it was ten years ago. I continue to believe, however, that senators take their responsibilities seriously enough to give at least a good look to a treaty that is manifestly in the national security interest of the United States. So it is incumbent on a president and his administration to try.

Where New START was concerned, we assumed that senators would be serious about the effort, and we made ourselves available throughout the summer and fall of 2010 to answer their questions. By the time the treaty entered into force, we had answered more than 1,000 questions for the record.

And we talked and talked and talked. We held more than twenty official hearings and briefings along with countless informal encounters—in senators' offices, with their staffers, in the corridors, in the cafeterias, wherever anybody had a question about New START, we were ready to talk.

We made sure that our briefings and talking points were consistent across the board because the last thing we needed were different nuances to which enemies of the treaty could point. It is natural that the Defense Department would emphasize different points from the State Department or intelligence agencies, but the body of the script had to hang together no matter what piece of it was being picked out. To achieve that consistency, I was glad to have a strongly led backstopping team that the authority of the White House was backing up. The team made sure that everybody was on the same page.

We were lucky early on that President Obama asked the vice president to lead the ratification effort—as noted previously, we called him our main "trail boss." With his long career in the Senate, Vice President Biden knew the importance of persistent engagement, and he used his talent for it to the max. I was impressed at how he brought senators from both sides of the aisle together in the Roosevelt Room of the White House and worked them. He made sure they knew that he and the president were listening to their concerns about nuclear modernization, from plutonium pit production to the next generation of strategic-strike submarines. Of course, the sites where they would be built was of great interest to the senators, and Biden was good at subtly making that case.

Vice President Biden let us, the experts, answer questions too, but not so much as to muddy the main message: The New START Treaty was the foundation on which modernization of the U.S. nuclear triad could take place without breaking the bank. Our nuclear forces, some of which were sixty years old, were chasing an ongoing modernization of Russian nuclear forces. We needed to modernize, all the while keeping Russian nuclear numbers under control. The New START Treaty was the means to achieve that goal.

Vice President Biden was an experienced operative on Capitol Hill, but he was also widely respected for his foreign and defense policy work over the years. He knew about nuclear weapons, and he knew about arms control; he knew what had worked in the past and what had not. The fact that he spoke with such authority was vital to the success of the process.

Vice President Biden had many responsibilities on behalf of the president, so I was thrilled that he gave New START ratification as much attention as he did, and also put one of his most experienced staff members, Brian McKeon, to stay on top of the day-to-day process. For the rest of us, the senior members of the delegation, we dropped everything to work on ratification full-time. To meet every senator and staffer who wanted to meet as many times as was necessary meant a full-time presence on Capitol Hill. Even if I couldn't be there every day, one of my colleagues from across the government was there. We ended up with a dedicated interagency team who were knowledgeable about the treaty and who had the authority to speak the right language to senators and make deals if necessary.

At the same time, we needed dedicated knowledge of the ratification process. Because moving treaties through the Senate had become so difficult in recent years, that knowledge had dissipated to the point that almost no one in the Obama administration understood the process from one end to the other. Brian McKeon, Vice President Biden's point person, knew the process from the Senate side, and was an experienced hand. Luckily, I had an experienced hand on the State Department side,

Terri Lodge, who had participated in the ratification of ten arms control treaties. She knew what breeds success and what breeds failure. Her earliest advice was to keep talking to anyone who would listen, our first and golden rule.

In addition, Lodge stressed absolute attention to detail and procedures, which is where a treaty can get tripped up in ratification. She worked with the State Department lawyers to ensure that the treaty package was full and complete on its way to the Senate. She sat for hours with Senate staffers and the lawyers to ensure that no language could creep into the Resolution of Ratification that would change the substance of the treaty. She stayed on top of the schedule of hearings and debate. She understood when and how the vote would be scheduled in a tight congressional calendar. And she knew the importance of outside influence to the process.

Importance of Outside Influence

With Terri Lodge, I spent a lot of time cultivating anyone who could help us on the outside—advocacy groups, religious organizations, eminent public figures, the media, the public—the more voices we had speaking up for the treaty, the better. As much as we were tramping the corridors of Capitol Hill, we were trekking the streets of Washington, DC, from K Street offices to the U.S. Catholic Bishops' headquarters at Catholic University. For some high-value targets such as the editorial board of the *Des Moines Register*, we took time to go out of town.

It was a prodigious effort, but it was worth it. A large number of eminent people, Republican and Democrat, spoke out to support New START. Religious organizations—Catholic, Baptist, Methodist, Evangelical, Quaker, and more—were urging support from Sunday pulpits. By the time the vote was in final preparation in the Senate, we had the public calling and mailing cards to their senators to support the treaty. Nuclear weapons arms control had come onto the radar scope of people in the heartlands. Unlike the mid-1940s through the 1960s, when the issue of nuclear weapons was part of mainstream consciousness, it wasn't easy to bring New START to the forefront, but we succeeded with hard work and a lot of allies.

In the years since New START ratification, social media have come to dominate the media and communications space. Often, they have contributed to divisions in the country as people stick more and more with their favored pundits and outlets. Would our old-fashioned footwork produce the same results today? I believe the answer is "no."

However, I do not believe that the speed and divisiveness of current media trends can only be a detriment to achieving big policy goals such as ratification of a treaty. Social media will be much more important to ratification in the future than they were in 2010. We will have to be constantly alert to negative trends picking up speed. At the same time, social media can be a huge force multiplier, allowing us to get messages out faster and to a wider audience than we accomplished with New START. I do not believe that social media condemn future treaties to failure, as long as we embrace the platforms for their advantages—and stay alert to what the algorithms are up to.

THE RUSSIANS, AGAIN

It may sound counterintuitive, but it is also important to keep the Russians informed and engaged during the ratification process. If something in the Resolution of Ratification takes them by surprise, they may treat it as more important than it actually is. I spent a lot of time, as did other senior people, talking to the Russians about the difference between legally binding language in the resolution, of which there was very little, and language that was a "sense of the Senate." On the day of the treaty vote, I took time to go on Russian national television to talk about the outcome and to underscore that the treaty had not been altered by the resolution. Even so, my counterpart called me the next day to complain about it, saying that it could poison their own process in the State Duma and Federation Council. We continued to stay in close touch with them throughout the Russian ratification to prevent that outcome. We succeeded in that regard.

IGNORE THE CASSANDRAS

One unexpected lesson that I learned is to pay no attention to the Cassandras. From the first moment I took the job in 2009, certain people on the inside kept up the refrain that "you will never get this treaty"—which surprised me given that their president was so committed to it. Even in the week of the final ratification vote, one prominent White House staffer told me, "You'll never succeed."

On the outside, some made the argument that Democratic presidents rarely succeed with arms control treaties. Some saw continuing opposition to arms control in important sectors of the American body politic and concluded that a new treaty would be impossible. Some saw fractiousness on Capitol Hill and predicted that we would never achieve Senate ratification.

Ironically, some outsiders who are big proponents of arms control thought the treaty was too small a step, in Washington parlance, a "nothing-burger." Even if we could get it, it wasn't good enough. More treaties would have to follow to fulfill President Obama's dream of a world without nuclear weapons. That went without saying, but we were focused on the fact that we needed immediate action to replace START. The treaty would not be the last word, but it was a necessary step taken. Why couldn't they celebrate that fact? I don't know.

I learned from that experience to be patient with cynicism and ignore doubts as much as humanly possible. I also felt it was my responsibility to shield the process from the naysayers, which is another reason that I kept up a drumbeat of optimism, first in Geneva, then during the ratification process. It cost me in terms of reputation—that "Pollyanna" thing again—but if I couldn't keep a positive face on the proceedings, who was going to do it?

WHEN YOU NEED HELP, GET IT

It's a given that arms control negotiators through the years have always dealt with stress. There is the stress of negotiating with the Russians, of dealing with Washington, and of running a delegation of simultaneously high-impact and high-maintenance people. All the moving parts are going fast. The stress of the New START negotiations gave me a dose of high blood pressure for the first time in my life.

As in other areas, I am not sure I gained any unique new insights into dealing with stress, but I did find out what worked for me: it was what had worked for me for a long time. My husband Ray and I have developed a kind of mutual admiration society and support system in our married life, and I knew that I could count on his advice. The fact that he well understood the behavior of the Washington bureaucracy was a great advantage, along with the fact that he knows how to get the best out of people. That he doesn't suffer fools gladly was an added bonus.

Although I didn't turn to him much in the early months, I found that I needed his advice often as the political pressures grew. We weren't discussing sensitive details of the negotiations, but he gave me good ideas about how to deal with certain individuals and get them over the hump of difficult issues. He was a great problem-solver where interagency tensions were an issue, and he had good advice about whom else I needed to talk to at high levels in Washington to get help. I am not sure that I would have gotten through the negotiations without Ray at the end of the secure phone. His contributions are not part of the official record, but he played a vital role in the success of the New START Treaty.

In the end, dumb luck was a factor in our success as in any human endeavor. If an Icelandic volcanic eruption hadn't kept the Russian team in Geneva for one more week, we may not have gotten the treaty package up to the Senate in time. If Michael Gordon's back hadn't gone out, the ratification vote might have been pushed off into an indefinite future. If President Medvedev had not decided on one occasion to stand up to Prime Minister Putin, we could still be arguing over missile defense.

We were lucky too to have a delegation that combined experienced hands with new talent. My senior team was unmatched in its experience and savvy, but some of the weapon systems operators had never met a Russian before. They proved to be the most natural negotiators that I have ever seen. Inside the delegation, people managed to get along despite some bad bouts of ill temper. We were lucky that the chemistry somehow worked.

But the most important factor by far was hard work—by a big team of talented people, with good political leadership backing them up. Hard work and good luck are the recipe that will bring us future treaties, too— as long as our political leaders are willing and step up to drive the process.

Epilogue

The New START Treaty came into force during a ceremony at the Munich Security Conference on February 5, 2011. Secretary of State Hillary Clinton and Minister of Foreign Affairs Sergei Lavrov signed the documents to record the entry into force, exchanging them afterwards with big smiles and applause all around. How long ago that seems. The Russian seizure of Crimea was three years away and some vestiges of the reset were still in operation, although Moscow was already complaining about U.S. interference in Russia's affairs, especially on human rights issues. Indeed, Lavrov had just made some grumpy comments to that effect in the Munich plenary meeting hall.

It seemed possible, however, that something of the "spirit of Geneva"—the practical, problem-solving relationship between the two delegations—could be preserved to advance U.S. and Russian interests in further strategic arms control. President Obama was still intent on making progress on nuclear reductions with another treaty, and the Russians continued to be concerned about U.S. missile defense developments, both in Europe and in the continental United States. They were not, as I had already discovered in Geneva, interested in pressing on with another treaty, but I thought that they could be convinced. Plenty of trends were emerging, especially new technologies, which could affect the nuclear balance. We both had an interest in maintaining that balance and the strategic stability that flowed from it.

So after the ceremony was over that day, Anatoly Antonov and I retired to the pub in the basement of the Hotel Bayerischer Hof, where the Munich Security Conference is held. We wanted to exchange a toast over the treaty's entry into force, but more importantly, we wanted to talk over next steps. Could we figure out a way to preserve the good working relationship that the two delegations had established at multiple levels, from the two of us, the chief negotiators, to the military experts who had a deep mutual understanding of the technical details? Neither of us knew whether our two capitals would support sustaining the relationship, but we agreed it was worth a try.

We talked about establishing a regular rhythm of meetings, perhaps twice a year, where the two delegations would come back together in Geneva for sustained discussion over one to two weeks. Such meetings could, we thought, be scheduled after the twice-yearly meetings of the Bilateral Consultative Commission, the New START implementing body, when the right people from both sides would be in Geneva anyway. The agenda would be agreed upon in advance, to address priority issues affecting strategic stability.

In my mind, these meetings would be different from the talks already underway, chaired by Undersecretary Ellen Tauscher and Deputy Foreign Minister Sergei Ryabkov, to discuss cooperation on missile defenses. The talks I had in mind would cover a wider range of topics, including the emergence of new technologies, such as hypersonic glide vehicles, and new arms control challenges, such as limiting warheads. Republicans in the U.S. Senate had already put us on notice that we must seek limits on Russian warheads in the next round of talks. Essentially, I thought a Geneva process could be used to build Russian interest in a new strategic arms reduction negotiation that would include new technologies and new problems that we had to tackle—warhead limits in particular.

While Antonov and I drank our Munich beer, a man sat down at the table next to us and opened a newspaper. He was so conspicuously close to us and so obviously intent on our conversation that Antonov said to me in a low voice, "Is he one of yours?" "No," I replied, "I don't think so. Is he one of yours?" He shrugged and we continued our conversation—there was nothing sensitive about it, except we knew we would have some convincing to do in Washington and Moscow.

To this day, I do not know whether that man was an intelligence operative or just some guy reading his newspaper. What I found out rather quickly, however, was that there was no interest in Washington in sustaining a Geneva process to scope out the next strategic reduction negotiation. Early on I approached Ellen Tauscher with the idea, and she told me gently that the attention now had to turn to the talks on missile defense, to try to develop some mutual understanding and cooperation with the Russians. Moreover, she said, that same set of talks would develop the strategic stability topics to prepare the way for the next negotiation. We will get the agenda for the next round ready to hand off to you, she said.

What ensued were good faith efforts by the United States to talk about missile defenses and to develop joint understanding and cooperation with the Russian Federation. Tauscher and her team were regularly accused on Capitol Hill of trying to limit U.S. missile defenses, but in fact they were wholly focused on these two tasks—joint understanding and cooperation. They also began to open discussion about new technologies and their effect on the strategic balance.

Meanwhile, I headed off to try to convince our NATO allies that it was time to limit warheads at the negotiating table, which meant that the allies would have to countenance Russian inspectors at NATO nuclear facilities on their territories. This proved to be a tough and eventually insurmountable task, as the NATO countries at the time showed little interest in joining such an effort. It was politically difficult for many of them, given public opposition to the NATO nuclear mission, and raised too many uncomfortable questions. But that is a story for another day.

As I think back over that period, I believe one of the problems that I did not foresee was how foreign the notion of long-standing talks in Geneva had become to the Washington community. During the Cold War, delegations had sat for long years in Stockholm or Vienna or Geneva, working out conventional as well as nuclear arms limitations. They also worked on missile defense issues and shaping European security arrangements. The Mutual Balanced Force Reduction (MBFR) talks went on from 1973 to 1989, eventually resulting in the Conventional Forces in Europe Treaty (CFE).

By 2011, such ideas were out of favor with the Washington establishment. Indeed, MBFR and other long-running negotiations had probably contributed to poisoning the well by making such slow progress. I should have taken more seriously the senior White House official who stopped me outside the Situation Room to ask whether I really needed to sit in Geneva with so many people for so long. At the time, I was perplexed that there wasn't a better understanding in the Obama administration of the advantages of an expert delegation with good, practical working links to its counterpart delegation. Now I know I shouldn't have downplayed his question.

What replaced delegation work were episodic visits to Moscow or other capitals in Europe, often Geneva, for a few days at a time, a few times a year. The results were not impressive, partially because the Russians became more and more recalcitrant but also because it was difficult to develop progress from one short meeting to the next. A couple days of plenaries to exchange talking points and briefings, perhaps with some smaller meetings woven in involving the delegation heads, are important to put ideas on the table. However, they cannot be used to develop joint long-term solutions to complex technical problems, simply because it is too difficult to sustain momentum during the intervening period—especially if difficult political issues begin to get in the way.

This outcome during the Obama years was the beginning of my conviction that "drive-by negotiations" do not succeed. That conviction has only been strengthened by the experience of the Trump years. In 2020, the two presidents, Putin and Trump, interacted at the highest level through frequent phone calls to put in place the major anchor points of a new agreement, including a freeze on all nuclear warheads and an extension of New START. However, their two teams did not interact in the substantive and consistent way that could have produced the necessary implementing measures, particularly a verification regime.

Instead, they got together for one or two days at a time in Geneva or Vienna, exchanged talking points, but never got down to the hard slog that produces substantive results. That hard slog cannot be avoided, and therefore I am sorry that the "spirit of Geneva" survives only in the decent working relationship between the two sides in the meetings of the Bilateral Consultative Commission. Perhaps it can be resurrected in future.

I believe that such resurrection will be necessary to tackle the tough issues that are raised by new technologies and by limits on warheads. It will also be necessary to try to control technologies that are not dependent on hardware such as missiles to perpetrate an attack—cyber weapons are a prime example. Joint development of the concepts of control, counting procedures when viable, and monitoring measures will all have to be done through detailed work among experts over a significant period of time.

For that reason, I will continue to press for bringing back sustained delegation work, not shying away from the necessity of sitting together for days, weeks, or even months to get the right results for U.S. national security.

These working relationships are not the same as friendships. We negotiate with friends and allies, but just as often we are negotiating with those whose beliefs and goals differ from our own—sometimes intensely so. Nevertheless, if we are to solve problems without recourse to military force, then we have to talk. That went for the Soviets during the Cold War, and it goes for the Russians now.

In coming times, we will be negotiating about weapons with the Chinese, and we will no doubt return to the table with the North Koreans and Iranians. On some dark day in the future, we may have to negotiate with a terrorist chieftain who is threatening us with a nuclear attack. To talk him off that precipice will require us to build some trust, some relationship. Hostage negotiators know this, but nuclear negotiators have never had to wrestle with such a problem.

Whether at the big table of strategic arms reduction talks or a small table, the principle is the same when facing a deadly terrorist: Only through the development of relationships in a negotiation do we hit that sweet spot where all parties can say yes.

President Biden and President Putin agreed to extend the New START Treaty on February 3, 2021. They did so according to terms already set in the treaty, which meant that it did not have to return to the U.S. Senate for a ratification process. It will remain in force until February 4, 2026, which gives ample time for the next negotiations to produce results.

Thus, the stage is set to tackle the tough issues that new technologies have brought us, as well as old problems that we have wanted to tackle for a long time, especially limiting warheads. Despite deep differences between Washington and Moscow on issues ranging from human rights to the state sovereignty of Russia's neighbors, we must continue to make progress in controlling and limiting nuclear weapons. It is our responsibility to humanity.

GLOSSARY

ballistic missile A missile that is initially rocket propelled and then follows a ballistic trajectory based on the force of gravity to deliver a nuclear or conventional warhead to a predetermined target. Such missiles are typically classified by the maximum distance they can travel. The New START Treaty addresses missiles with a range in excess of 5500 km while the Intermediate-Range Nuclear Forces (INF) Treaty addressed those with ranges between 500 and 5500 km.

bomber An aircraft designed to drop bombs on its targets from above or deliver air-launched missiles from a stand-off distance; strategic heavy bombers can fly to intercontinental ranges above 8,000 kilometers to deliver nuclear or conventional armaments.

conventional armaments Types of weapons that are not chemical, biological, radiological, or nuclear (CBRN) weapons.

conversion or elimination A verifiable procedure under which a nuclear launcher or delivery vehicle is either converted for conventional non-nuclear payloads or eliminated from the arsenal.

cruise missile A self-propelled, guided, maneuverable missile that is usually low-flying and difficult to detect and may be launched from land, aircraft, surface ships, or submarines to deliver a warhead over long distances with precision.

delivery vehicle A ballistic or cruise missile, or a bomber, designed to carry a nuclear weapon.

deployed A weapon system or part of a weapon system (warhead, delivery vehicle, launcher) that is operationally ready to launch to a target and not designated for test, training, or space launch.

front section The section at the top of the missile that carries reentry vehicles containing nuclear warheads and conventional penetration aids such as decoys.

ICBM An intercontinental ballistic missile with a range greater than 5,500 kilometers.

launcher A system designed to contain a missile for launch; if mobile, it is used for both transport and launch.

monitoring Activities conducted to obtain, evaluate, and coordinate information from data exchanges, notifications, ground inspection procedures, and National Technical Means (NTM).

missile defense Technology and systems designed to detect, track, and intercept missiles, preventing them from arriving at their targets.

missile silo An underground cylindrical facility designed to contain, protect, and launch a deployed ICBM.

NTM National technical means of verification, which include satellites and aircraft owned by individual treaty parties, as well as radars. These collect imagery and data that are relevant to monitoring a treaty. For that purpose, treaty parties agree not to interfere with the NTM of other parties.

new type A new and improved generation of a missile that is already limited under a treaty.

new kind A new missile or weapon concept that does not fit the limits defined under a treaty.

non-deployed A missile launcher or a bomber that is in storage, maintenance, or used solely for tests and training or for space launch.

reentry vehicle A device in the front section of an intercontinental missile designed to carry and protect warheads, ensuring they survive reentry through the dense layers of Earth's atmosphere and detonate on target.

SLBM A submarine-launched ballistic missile, with a range greater than 5,500 kilometers.

strategic arms Long-range weapons capable of hitting targets at ranges greater than 5,500 kilometers. They can carry conventional armaments ("strategic conventional missiles"), but they normally carry nuclear payloads ("strategic nuclear missiles").

telemetry Performance data originating from a missile during flight tests that is broadcast for recovery and analysis.

throw-weight Maximum lift capability or payload of a missile, which determines the number and type of warheads it can carry.

unique identifier (UID) A non-repeating set of letters and digits used to identify and track missiles and bombers through treaty notifications and on-site inspections.

verification The analytical policy-based process to confirm a party's compliance with treaty obligations, including the validity of previously made declarations of weapon system status, the results from on-site inspections and NTM.

warhead An explosive device, carried and delivered by a missile or bomber that can be either nuclear or conventional.

weapons of mass destruction Chemical, biological, radiological, or nuclear (CBRN) weapons that are capable of inflicting immense, indiscriminate damage and causing loss of life.

INDEX

About the Author

Rose Gottemoeller is the Frank E. and Arthur W. Payne Distinguished Lecturer at Stanford University's Freeman Spogli Institute for International Studies and its Center for International Security and Cooperation. She is also a research fellow at the Hoover Institution.

Before joining Stanford, Gottemoeller was the Deputy Secretary General of NATO from 2016 to 2019, where she helped to drive forward NATO's adaptation to new security challenges in Europe and in the fight against terrorism. Prior to NATO, she served for nearly five years as the Under Secretary for Arms Control and International Security at the U.S. Department of State, advising the Secretary of State on arms control, nonproliferation and political-military affairs. While Assistant Secretary of State for Arms Control, Verification and Compliance in 2009 and 2010, she was the chief US negotiator of the New Strategic Arms Reduction Treaty (New START) with the Russian Federation.

Before this government service, she was a senior associate with the Carnegie Endowment for International Peace, with joint appointments to the Nonproliferation and Russia programs. She served as the Director of the Carnegie Moscow Center from 2006 to 2008 and is currently a nonresident fellow in Carnegie's Nuclear Policy Program.

Praise for the Book

"As advances in technology usher in a new age of weaponry, future negotiators would benefit from reading Rose Gottemoeller's memoir of the process leading to the most significant arms control agreement of recent decades."

—Henry Kissinger, former U.S. Secretary of State

* * * * * * *

"Rose Gottemoeller's book on the New START negotiations is the definitive book on this treaty or indeed, any of the nuclear treaties with the Soviet Union or Russia. These treaties played a key role in keeping the hostility between the United States and the Soviet Union from breaking out into a civilization-ending war. But her story of the New START negotiation is no dry academic treatise. She tells with wit and charm the human story of the negotiators, as well as the critical issues involved. Rose's book is an important and well-told story about the last nuclear treaty negotiated between the US and Russia."

—William J. Perry, former U.S. Secretary of Defense

* * * * * * *

"This book is important, but not just because it tells you about a very significant past, but also because it helps you understand the future."

— George Shultz, former U.S. Secretary of State

* * * * * * *

"The world has entered into a new era of increased nuclear risks. Rising great power tensions, compressed decision time for leaders and new technologies like cyber are increasing the chances of war by blunder. At this moment when the need to restore skillful and creative diplomacy to reduce nuclear perils is urgent, Rose Gottemoeller's memoir is timely and instructive. As the chief U.S. negotiator of the New START Treaty, her insights–offered with humility, candor and humor–give readers a front row and personal view of what it takes to negotiate a complex nuclear agreement. Leading the U.S. negotiating team (first time by a woman), engaging the Russians, navigating Washington politics at the highest level and laying the foundation for ratification by the Senate are all crucial parts of the job. Rose has it exactly right about the critical importance for the Congress to be engaged and consulted by the Executive Branch in its "Advice" role long before Senate "Consent" is requested. Our leaders have no more important duty than to protect our nation from nuclear catastrophe. This memoir by one of our most skilled and respected diplomats provides both inspiration and valuable lessons for those who will follow in her shoes with this enormous responsibility."

–Sam Nunn, Chairman of the Board
of the Nuclear Threat Initiative

* * * * * * * *

"*Negotiating the New START Treaty* provides a deeply informed, highly readable, and timely analysis of one of the most important nuclear treaties in recent history. Rose Gottemoeller, one of America's foremost arms control experts, takes the reader behind closed doors in Europe and the United States. She dives into every stage of the painstaking consultations between the U.S. and Russian delegations in 2009 and 2010. Gottemoeller's sweeping historical narrative and personal reflections, combined with her evident wisdom and political objectivity, provide unique insight into the continued threat of nuclear proliferation to global security. This book is an invaluable guide for understanding the craft of arms control negotiations, as well as the critical role and responsibility of skillful, knowledgeable, and determined negotiators."

–Fiona Hill, Senior Fellow, Foreign Policy Program,
The Brookings Institution

* * * * * * * *

"Rose Gottemoeller, one of the world's most respected international security experts, chronicles in this remarkable book invaluable personal reflections and authoritative insights gained as a leader in America's most important chapter in recent arms control history— the New START Treaty. What makes this such a timely offering is the wisdom born of success that can help guide Washington's next phase of critical negotiations with Moscow. This extraordinary firsthand account is indispensable reading of arguably the most important national security issue of our time."

— Jon Huntsman, former Governor of Utah,
former U.S. Ambassador to China, Russia, and Singapore

CAMBRIA RAPID COMMUNICATIONS IN CONFLICT AND SECURITY (RCCS) SERIES

General Editor: Geoffrey R. H. Burn

The aim of the RCCS series is to provide policy makers, practitioners, analysts, and academics with in-depth analysis of fast-moving topics that require urgent yet informed debate. Since its launch in October 2015, the RCCS series has the following book publications:

- *A New Strategy for Complex Warfare: Combined Effects in East Asia* by Thomas A. Drohan

- *US National Security: New Threats, Old Realities* by Paul R. Viotti

- *Security Forces in African States: Cases and Assessment* edited by Paul Shemella and Nicholas Tomb

- *Trust and Distrust in Sino-American Relations: Challenge and Opportunity* by Steve Chan

- *The Gathering Pacific Storm: Emerging US-China Strategic Competition in Defense Technological and Industrial Development* edited by Tai Ming Cheung and Thomas G. Mahnken

- *Military Strategy for the 21st Century: People, Connectivity, and Competition* by Charles Cleveland, Benjamin Jensen, Susan Bryant, and Arnel David

- *Ensuring National Government Stability After US Counterinsurgency Operations: The Critical Measure of Success* by Dallas E. Shaw Jr.

- *Reassessing U.S. Nuclear Strategy* by David W. Kearn, Jr.

- *Deglobalization and International Security* by T. X. Hammes

- *American Foreign Policy and National Security* by Paul R. Viotti

- *Make America First Again: Grand Strategy Analysis and the Trump Administration* by Jacob Shively
- *Learning from Russia's Recent Wars: Why, Where, and When Russia Might Strike Next* by Neal G. Jesse
- *Restoring Thucydides: Testing Familiar Lessons and Deriving New Ones* by Andrew R. Novo and Jay M. Parker
- *Net Assessment and Military Strategy: Retrospective and Prospective Essays* edited by Thomas G. Mahnken, with an introduction by Andrew W. Marshall
- *Deterrence by Denial: Theory and Practice* edited by Alex S. Wilner and Andreas Wenger
- *Negotiating the New START Treaty* by Rose Gottemoeller

For more information, visit www.cambriapress.com.